Structuring Your Res

Structuring Your Research Thesis

Susan Carter
Frances Kelly
Ian Brailsford

palgrave
macmillan

Published 2012 by
PALGRAVE MACMILLAN

Palgrave Macmillan in the UK is an imprint of Macmillan Publishers Limited,
registered in England, company number 785998, of Houndmills, Basingstoke,
Hampshire RG21 6XS.

Palgrave Macmillan in the US is a division of St Martin's Press LLC,
175 Fifth Avenue, New York, NY 10010.

Palgrave Macmillan is the global academic imprint of the above companies
and has companies and representatives throughout the world.

Palgrave® and Macmillan® are registered trademarks in the United States,
the United Kingdom, Europe and other countries

ISBN 978-0-230-30813-8

This book is printed on paper suitable for recycling and made from fully
managed and sustained forest sources. Logging, pulping and manufacturing
processes are expected to conform to the environmental regulations of the
country of origin.

A catalogue record for this book is available from the British Library.

A catalog record for this book is available from the Library of Congress.

10   9   8   7   6   5   4   3   2   1
21 20 19 18 17 16 15 14 13 12

Printed and bound in China

Contents

Acknowledgements

● Students

We are grateful to the thesis-writing students whose conversations over structuring challenges inspired this book, and the participants in our survey who gave insight. Thesis-writing students in our many classroom sessions on structuring a thesis enabled us to refine and consolidate our ideas on the process, the product, why structure is difficult and what approaches might be useful. We thank our students, some of whom are now colleagues.

● Colleagues

We are also indebted to generous colleagues who contributed their lively personal stories, breathing more life into our text: Ann Hutchison, Jackie Kidd, Nicholas Rowe, and Tony Stroobant. We thank the Centre for Academic Development for sustaining collegiality and funding. The Academic Women Writers Group should be mentioned for their ongoing support with thinking and writing. Palgrave Macmillan editorial staff, especially Suzannah Burywood and Jennifer Schmidt, have been encouraging and helpful with their direction. Ann Edmondson was diligently attentive in proofing suggestions as we went into print.

And we also thank each other for sharing the journey.

Preface: Our Reader and Your Readers

Our reader

The intended reader of this book is the thesis writer who is struggling with the structure of their thesis. Many students struggle, despite the fact that thesis writers are, for the most part, crème-de-la-crème students, those who excelled in their taught courses. One of the main differences between excelling in taught courses and writing a thesis is that taught courses have been mapped out by the lecturer and already designed to make sense before students arrive. Considerable thought has gone into the logical structure of the course materials, ideas and progressions. However, the structural work of the thesis must be done by the thesis author. A supervisor may help with some decisions, but the responsibility for the structure and for its logical progression and cohesion rests with the thesis candidate. For some students the task is relatively straightforward whereas others find themselves in a rampant jungle without a map. In this unforgiving terrain, thesis ideas multiply, tangle together, morph and blend: maintaining a sense of order and logic can be an epic battle of will.

This book, informed by a survey of graduate student experiences, was prompted by our observations, as learning advisors, of the problems students have with structuring their thesis. Other authors who have investigated the graduate student experience confirm our opinion. Doctoral candidates can find themselves with 'large quantities of disparate data and little developed idea about how to fit it all together, or to make meaning from it' (Wisker, 2001, p. 143). Amassing a plethora of interesting data may make it even harder to produce the finished thesis because these data need to be ordered and structured. Planning the thesis structure seemingly requires 'heroic optimism' (Dunleavy, 2003, p. 43). Facts need to be given a story line so that they become coherent, yet 'it is surprisingly easy to lose track of the central thread' (Swetnam, 2003, p. 108). The initial absence of a presentation plan is the 'one major difficulty students have' (Rudestam and Newton, 2001, p. 117). And there are 'classic pitfalls in research design,' including 'putting the cart before the horse', 'great expectations', and 'sand through the fingers' (Rugg and Petre, 2005, p. 153). Indeed, for many doctoral candidates, the need to structure the written account – the thesis – may be more of a challenge than the doctoral research itself (Carter, 2009).

On a more encouraging note, the structuring process does more than simply order material. The task of structuring is unavoidable, yet the process establishes authorial control: the result of a sound structure is more than a sum of the parts. Writing of paragraph clarity, Davis and McKay note that '[T]he clarity of ... structure has the strategic effect of making [the paragraph] seem authoritative. In this sense a text's structural features are simultaneously strategic' (Davis and McKay, 1996, p. 3). Control over structure gives authority to prose. Through its emphasis, structure also covertly suggests the values of the author, and self-awareness of their own context. The doctoral thesis gives shape to an original idea. Shaping requires design: the structure of the thesis is different from the structure of the research. The research has its own order, but the thesis author will need to consider the discipline-specific conventions of writing, the regulatory requirements of a thesis and the readerly requirements of the examiner. Yet there is authorial power in the writing process, with a wide scope for originality. The structure of the research is driven by methodological consideration, and by the dictates of time; the structure of the writing can be designed to maximize the potential of the research findings. This book suggests how to design a structure that foregrounds the significance of your research work.

Many of those students who struggle with thesis design will be candidates in arts, law, the humanities and social sciences (including health systems, education and business studies) whose research work is qualitative 'soft' science because these disciplines and their research theses are generally non-formulaic. It is useful at this juncture to consider the work on 'academic tribes and territories' (Becher and Trowler,

2001). Doctoral theses can be divided into four quadrants: applied social sciences (such as education); technologies (such as mechanical engineering); humanities and pure social sciences (such as history and anthropology); and finally pure sciences (such as physics) (Becher, 1994). Doctoral students in the pure or hard sciences typically present their thesis data in a structured format that is universally accepted; doctoral students working in the other three quadrants have the blessing (or the curse) of more freedom to mould their thesis structure as they see fit.

A student in our graduate survey, for instance, commented that 'as my work is philosophical, there are many factors that all support one another, so it is difficult to know which one to start with, as it is all rather circular.' Writing on research methods for the arts and humanities, Wisker (2001, p. 266) notes that: 'Much creative work takes place in the intersection of critical perspectives, cultural contexts and the personal.' This intersection is a busy one where discourses collide and must be fitted together with careful deliberation. The personal brings its own integrity to the exegetical thesis, but also its own idiosyncrasies. Fitting the personal – uniquely shaped – into the confines of the thesis genre – which is convention based – requires careful tailoring. The thesis is the potential entry point to a future academic career, so the identity of the author, constructed through the writing, is important. The desired values underpinning the research need to inhere in the structure.

Although one student in our survey reflected that '[structure is] a very intangible thing that you can only talk about once it is done and complete; during the process it's so fluid that it's hard to articulate upon', here we broach the topic overtly, aiming to make the process more conceivable. To some extent this student is correct, and we acknowledge that for many students structure may only become fully clear to them in the final process of writing, or on completion, or even only on re-reading it years after completion. For some students, writing is part of the research methodology, the medium enabling exegetical thought. This book aims to provide more clarity about structuring choices earlier in the process. We include reflections on the structuring of the thesis by successful candidates in non-formulaic disciplines.

For many thesis writers, ideas on structure remain provisional well into the process, and indeed, another graduate student described the difficulty of structuring as the fact that 'it feels like committing to a particular structure is like ruling out many equally interesting and viable (possibly more viable!) parallel universes.' For others, it may seem that each component of their original thesis design has in fact already been investigated once they read in more depth. Nicholas tells his story of persevering through the blind alleys of a practice-based doctorate until he found his research question:

> I spent the first two years of my thesis flailing passionately through different areas of literature, endlessly discovering that what I thought would be my contribution to knowledge on dance had already been discussed elsewhere. These realizations were very demoralizing and sat on my shoulder like a nagging old parrot, constantly reinforcing a sense that I really didn't have an original thought in my head and that perhaps academic research wasn't really for me. I came to fear literature.
>
> Ultimately the thing that got me through this was remaining sensually, socially and politically immersed in my subject area; in the dance scene of the Occupied Palestinian Territories. While I couldn't clearly articulate a research idea that I thought was both unique and valuable in the first two doctoral years, an ephemeral sense that there was an important study to be done there kept me hungry to conduct research and write it up for the world to see. When I did gain some clarity on my research quest(ion), it came charging through like a snorting bull demanding to be followed, not led. It's not that everything became clear at that point and that I then had an easy ride into the final submission of my thesis. So much information on the impact of cultural trauma on dance in the Occupied Palestinian Territories still had to be deciphered, analysed, evaluated, edited, gained and abandoned.
>
> Structuring the mountain of ideas that emerged into a coherent whole remained a huge challenge. But at least through the identification of a clear, valuable and unique research quest(ion), the demoralizing uncertainty was gone.

It's odd in retrospect, because I had of course provided research questions in the initial proposals and reports to my supervisor and university. But in my heart I had known them to be a bit of a bluff. They were questions that sounded important but were ultimately too large for me to ever answer or too small to be of any use. They felt like something to just buy me time, but I guess they also proved to be some sort of lighthouse when I felt like a boat lost in a fog. Perhaps as a result of the doctoral process I've come to fall in love with really good questions. They can make life so easy.

Performance-based doctoral theses face particular challenges in how the written work relates to the performance (or exhibition) when the culture and pedagogy of one may seem at loggerheads with those of the other. Nicholas' experience demonstrates that sometimes you need to trust your own instincts and patiently keep working until you find clarity. Once the main research questions are found, however, it may still be difficult to decide on the order, and on the emphasis. Yet, since thesis writers do need to make decisions, and may be under external pressures to complete the doctorate within a shorter time than the full exploration of available universes would require, in the meantime it is worth remembering that a revision of structure (and of emphasis) lies open as an option for a published version once the thesis is complete. We hope that some of what follows will help in the meantime towards that first stage, the thesis completion. To this end, this book provides a set of models to assist your decision-making about thesis structure.

Following the introduction, which covers a range of preliminary issues and sketches some of the principles involved in the main chapters, the book comprises three parts. Successful structuring of a thesis is achieved at three different levels:

1   the ordering of material,
2   the emphasis achieved through the proportioning of material, and
2   the finer structural detail that allows the parts to cohere.

Thus, the three chapters of the book deal with ordering, emphasis and cohesion, each made up of subtopics. It would be possible, then, to read this book at the beginning of the doctoral project and follow its suggestions as navigational markers through the wilderness of the thesis process. This makes sense because ordering is an early consideration regarding thesis layout, followed by the need to emphasize the themes that are to be more significant over the less significant ones, and with the need for coherence and cohesion before submission. Indeed, anyone who is in the middle of their doctorate and finding structure problematic might apply these approaches in the hope that something here will give them insight into a viable structure that will satisfy their examiners, even if it might not be the structure of the book that will convey their thoughts to the world in later publication. We hope, too, that readers well into the thesis process and still unsure of their final structure will find what works for them amongst a wide smorgasbord of suggestions.

Supervisors are also likely to find the book useful in anatomizing the dimensions of the structuring process. We hope that it will enable clearer discussions to take place around structure as a result of the smorgasbord of approache that this book brings to thesis decision-making.

Finally, any one of the chapters may seem more pertinent than others due to the individual nature of each thesis project. Because the book addresses the generic requirements of the written thesis and is not discipline-focussed, you may find some of the detail occasionally less relevant to your particular project.

● Your readers

Publication beyond the confines of the thesis may be your ultimate desire for your research output, but the first part of the process is finishing that thesis and passing the doctoral examination itself. The primary reader of the thesis is the examiner, who must be satisfied that regulatory requirements have been met. The examiner, the imagined reader or The Reader has needs that are generated by their responsibility: they must be able to sign off the thesis as complying with these expectations. A doctoral thesis generally must meet a fairly consistent set of criteria. With slight institutional variations of formal language, a doctoral thesis:

- is an original contribution to knowledge or understanding in its field and
- meets internationally recognized standards for such work and
- demonstrates knowledge of the literature relevant to the subject and the field or fields from which the subject belongs, and the ability to exercise critical and analytical judgement of it, and
- is satisfactory in its methodology, in the quality and coherence of its written expression, and in its scholarly presentation and format. (University of Auckland, 2011, pp. 7–8)

In different countries, and in different institutions within countries, there will be found different processes of examination, usually involving committees who oversee the process. Some institutions have an oral examination, and practices vary between private and public examination. The role of the supervisor in the process may vary. The requirement for examiners to be external from the institution may vary. However, inevitably, the earliest readers of your thesis will be those charged with examining it.

An examiner is likely to feel the weight of their responsibility in making judgment and constructive comments on the thesis. These requirements, and the labours of the unknown examiner, often reading in the evening after a hard day's work, should inform decisions about structure. The thesis has a necessarily critical reader, but one whose criteria are known, so that their needs can be met and anxiety allayed. To underscore this point, this book has the thesis writer as an intended reader, but there is another reader, the examiner, who is also constantly in mind. For this reason, we consider the thesis reader's needs regarding the material of each chapter, including comments from examiners as to how they find, see and evaluate structure. Before we approach order, emphasis and cohesion, we introduce the overall framework that affects structuring decisions.

Introduction: Framework

All writing is validated in terms of how well it addresses its audience. We have written this book following our work with doctoral students and our recognition of the challenge of publication. Similar doctoral candidates of the future make up our audience. Like others' theses, yours must speak to its audience, addressing their needs, anxieties and expectations. As you start working and writing your thesis proposal, initial ideas will develop further and these present a set of challenges, or at least decisions that need to be made. The proposal stage has been likened to a 'trial run' (Sternberg, 1981, p. 73) for structuring the doctoral thesis. How many chapters should you have in your thesis? Must all the chapters be of a similar size? Will you provide the literature review as a separate chapter, or embed it throughout the thesis? How much explaining and framing will be done generally in the introduction, and how much will be done at chapter level? How many levels of subtitling will work best to convey your ideas? Should the thesis have internal divisions within it rather than conventional chapter ones? These are questions of structure: the overall shape of the thesis, its organization, its internal dimensions and parts, its plan and duration, and its proportions.

At the same time as these questions are being raised, most thoughtful candidates are acutely aware that they are embarking on a different writing project from anything that they have ever done before. Several useful handbooks give guidance as to the genre of the thesis. Examiners will need to confirm that you demonstrate your awareness of writing in this genre. We cite several handbooks here as appropriate (including Dunleavy, 2003; Murray, 2011; Phillips and Pugh, 2001; Wisker, 2001). Of these, Dunleavy focuses most overtly on the structuring process, offering a good practical working model that is well worth consideration. However, in our experience many doctoral authors are persuaded by loyalty to their research material to resist the good workable standard model, or at least to want to elaborate or adapt it rather drastically.

Jacqui, for instance, reflected on the way that her data were so sensitive that her thesis structure had to be changed so that the whole stories she obtained from her participants would be represented, privileging their voices and accounts more than the analysis she imposed on them.

My research was in the sensitive area of nurses who have experienced a mental illness. I was using a highly qualitative methodology which involved collecting stories from my participants, and writing emotional stories and poems as a part of my analysis. The combination of the sensitivity of the topic and the creative methodology meant that the traditional thesis structure was unlikely to work for my thesis. The particular issue I faced was how to re-present the stories I was given as data in such a way that treated the participants with care, while allowing me the space I needed to analyse the stories, and that also demonstrated methodological rigour.

It took lots of supervision sessions and many trials of different structures before I settled on one that I am still pleased with, several years later. I included the participants' stories, in their entirety, in my thesis. I had 18 stories, which was about 32,000 words, so I applied to the university for permission to submit a longer-than-usual thesis. The inclusion of the nurses' stories demonstrated respect; it meant that they weren't chopped up and used only from my perspective – the nurses retained their own voice in my work. It also meant that my examiners and readers could access the data and draw their own conclusions about my analysis. Making the process of analysis explicit is a vital part of demonstrating quality research, and is particularly important in the creative qualitative methodologies.

I also deliberately used the stories to interrupt the academic voice in my final structure choice. I was wary of creating a document that was theoretical and therefore removed from the reality of life as experienced by the nurses, so I carefully placed their stories between chapters, making sure that their 'real life' voices disrupted the flow of academic reading and required readers to stop and reflect on lived experience, or flick through pages to relocate the academic voice.

My literature review followed the pattern of the interposed stories and analysis. I used a broad literature review in the second chapter to position my research, but the more specific literature was introduced at the end of the three findings' chapters in response to the issues that were raised by my participants. This is a common approach in qualitative methodologies such as grounded theory, where the data guides the direction of the research. It worked well to reinforce my position as 'student' listening to the experiences of my participants, and not only made the thesis easier to read by breaking up the long and dense parts of my writing, but overtly valued the nurses' voices.

Jacqui's experience is not unusual in qualitative research theses because this method of gathering data values the phenomenology of the participants, giving deeper understandings to their experiences. Similarly, in exegetical theses – ones that unpack and interpret some aspect of the world – the structure may be tantamount to the methodology. Along with the voice of the prose, which establishes academic identity, structure will subtly suggest the values that underpin the research through the emphasis of its form. Structure *shapes* thought.

The thesis presents thought, some of which is original, within a supportive framework of institutional convention. The writer is aware of academic discipline. Most theses are situated within one discipline, but increasing numbers are interdisciplinary. The third cycle of the Bologna Process (Department for Education and Skills, 2007) emphasizes the benefits of interdisciplinary research, extolling universities as the organizations to foster this: the world is undisciplined and perhaps doctoral research should be more about the world than about the conventions. Yet two things must happen even in an interdisciplinary thesis: there must be a flaring spark of originality and a solid framework evidencing academic expertise. How greatly can that spark be fanned without risk of burning down the supporting framework of discipline scholarship? Awareness of discipline conventions must be demonstrated, along with awareness of the thesis genre.

A doctoral thesis changes the world. To some extent the thesis is an example of effective, and indeed, affective, language where words do something (Austin, 1975) rather than just talking about something. Austin's examples of how to do things with language are taken from words like 'I do' in the marriage ceremony, or 'not guilty' in a court room. The completion of the thesis, similarly, makes a real change in the world: it will change both the status of its author and the state of the disciplinary discourse. Structuring the thesis is part of this transformational writing process. Its significance for some authors deepens the difficulty of choice. Critical theory may prompt you to leave the conventional structural thesis shape in order to ensure that form follows function. Allegiance to your subject might also suggest creative possibilities for non-conventional structure. At the same time, it is good to have a firm grasp on what a thesis is and what it does so that you ensure your success. You will need to negotiate the tension between thesis genre conventions (established within the walls of the university) and the value systems of your unique topic (belonging to the chaos of the world). You are the diplomat who crosses boundaries and pulls conflicting cultures into a functional working relationship with each other to the mutual benefit of both.

Structure involves order, emphasis and cohesion. For thesis writers, order is most pressing. How will the contents page show logical order? When materials, ideas, and data develop with what may seem like fervid fertility, figuring out where material belongs best in the written thesis can be challenging. Parry (2007, p. 83) quotes a doctoral student describing difficulty structuring their thesis until they eventually 'met someone who said, "look, you've got to adopt one angle and chop off a lot of the not-so-related stuff". It's been a lot easier since then.' Battle metaphors and 'chopping off' seem appropriate; it may feel like doing violence to the multidimensional material to batter it into one finite form. Sometimes everything is so interrelated that separation seems like mutilation.

Perhaps it is not surprising that it is difficult to identify the boundaries of the thesis perimeter since they do not exist, but rather, they need to be created, justified and maintained by the thesis author. The process is somewhat arbitrary. Your thoughts, data and material may have the potential for several different theses, and yet you must choose which one you will produce. This is a little like choosing a Turkish carpet: the selection may be roughly similar, and precisely which single one's patterns, colours, size and price (in terms of time rather than money) you settle upon can seem overwhelming. In the end, it will be your task to make choices and then make them work cohesively. You can have only one thesis.

Cohesion is established structurally through order and proportion, yet this needs to be maintained with linguistic devices. These may be undetectable if they function well, just as the mechanic's careful tinkering is not evident once the car is purring along the highway. The cohesive manipulation of structural language should consciously synchronize with the overall design. Architectural principles apply: order and proportion give function and stability to the text, but a cohesive design establishes the identity and presence of the construction.

For some non-formulaic theses, structure will be bound together with content. It may be that the material of the thesis yields the structural patterning from its own deeper levels. The symbolism of the subject, the subjective stance of the author, the metaphors of a text, the mindset of the people under investigation or their theoretical models are but a few examples of the topic's potential to provide a structure modelled on the material. We give concrete examples below (Chapter 3), but suggest that all of the approaches work best when they resonate meaningfully with your own unique material. Some approaches may be irrelevant, but we hope that something here will be useful. Structure could become a significant dimension of the creativity of your writing production. A thesis need not aspire to being a work of art, yet it does need to convince examiners that it is an adequate example of the genre.

● Escape clause

The actual task of writing a thesis requires careful crafting to ensure balance and proportion. Everything that follows is prefaced by this qualification: your thesis does not need to be a magnum opus. You do not need to save the world by writing it, nor do you need to produce perfection. You won't produce perfection: almost every thesis writer has their own anecdote about the typos they found in the final edition despite an editing effort of mammoth proportions. Further, as you look at other examples of theses, you are likely to be struck at times by how flat-footed they are, how many are the small imperfections of one kind or another, and how few and far between are your moments of real interest and admiration. The advice, then, is to be practical. You need to finish the thesis but its completion is likely to be just another milestone in the trajectory of your research investigation. We stress that you should take the most direct route to a good submitted thesis: go the short way round the barn whenever you can figure out which way that is. However, those who find that structure is a challenge will find a set of suggestions in this book to hone their decision-making abilities around structuring issues.

● Layout of this book

The book takes a series of approaches to the structuring issues that we have built into three central chapters: order, emphasis and cohesion, with acknowledgment of the reader's needs in each instance. To some extent the division of the three main sections is arbitrary in that the levels of structure work together. Order is perhaps the most evident step in structure, given that written work is linear.

In Chapter 1, we first look at the principle behind the order in which parts of the thesis appear: the generic movement of the thesis, the moves that every thesis must demonstrate to satisfy examiners. These are usually established in the thesis introduction. We then focus on order within the thesis. Our suggestions about the implications of emphasis are based on practical experience.

We suggest a basic structural model to set alongside your own and discuss what it offers those for whom such a basic formula is not ideal. There are some moves that every thesis will make. Once you have identified what these are, you can decide where in your own work you are likely to make them. If you recognize that some of the thesis moves will be made somewhat unusually in your work, you are in a stronger position to defend your choices in your methodology section, however you present it.

We then suggest that you experiment with cognitive cartography, developing a mind-map into a diagrammatic model, or set of possible models, drawn out visually on the page. Mind-mapping allows you to identify the features that will be part of your work by spreading them onto a page so that the larger overview is visible in a non-hierarchical order. Modelling makes a deliberate pattern of the nouns that proliferate on your mind-map and begins to apply structure to these nouns. Some of the verb ideas that exist between the mind-map's nouns may be the most important arguments of your thesis and thus most important to structure; these will influence the diagram. We then look at Davis and McKay's grid model (Davis and McKay, 1996) as an example of the way diagrams convey the meaning you will make of the facts in your work. Shifting from vertical to horizontal (or vice versa) in the diagram of your model will shift the privileging of content.

At this stage we turn to the parts of the thesis that convey the genre moves. We mention the questions of where literature will be reviewed, where methodology will be shown, and the need to distinguish broad general material from detailed. We then discuss the contents page, one space that directly displays the structure of the thesis. There are many ways to build this page, and each has its advantages and disadvantages. Your discipline, epistemology and individual preference, even your individual strengths and weaknesses, will influence your contents page layout. Translating your diagrammatic model to a contents page gives another lens to the structuring process.

Observing that two interconnected processes (writing and planning) take the thesis structuring forward, we then move on to mnemonic theory from the past. Mnemonic theory offers another slant that literalizes the metaphor of writing structure as building structure. Mnemonic principles come from an essentially pre-literate era and were formulated and refined to enable the memory to be developed; in other words, this system was designed to enable extensive material to be held in the mind rather than on the page (or screen). Mnemonics does this through ordering the material to be remembered and providing vivid images at strategic points: order is the method of mnemonics, which is what makes the theory useful to thesis writers.

In Chapter 2 on emphasis and proportion, we introduce a quantitative approach to the thesis. It can be hard to judge how much detail and explanation is necessary; thinking quantitatively can help delimitation. We suggest ways to accommodate the need for unwieldy bulk in the thesis. We consider the difficulties when there are multiple levels of depth and voice, such as when the thesis investigates one period's representation of an earlier one, using current theory as well as theory that is contemporary with both periods. Then we review some of the grammatical principles that establish emphasis in writing.

In Chapter 3, we begin our discussion of structural cohesion by unpacking the commonplace notion that every thesis tells a story. Stories have their own conventions, and overt consideration of these may help you control the story of your thesis by using narrative conventions and the terms that belong to a specific genre. Even if you do not decide to actively employ these conventions, you should avoid abusing them.

Because it makes use of the complex semiotics of poetic language, metaphor can also be a strong structuring device. Metaphors that have a cultural underpinning enable a researcher to inhabit a social or cultural space simultaneously with their academic one. Cultural metaphors demonstrate the way that metaphor can contribute to methodology, and our examples make explicit the deep-level functioning of metaphor to carry one set of connotative meaning into another field. Finally, we pay attention to the joinery of the thesis, providing a checklist of strategies for achieving this while suggesting that this work can be used to inculcate and underscore the values that are important to your work.

Each approach concludes with a suggestion of how you might apply this approach to your own work. If structure is a burning issue, then something here should be of use. Even if it is not foremost in your current goals and challenges, if you have days when you feel that you need re-inspiration then you could try some of these options so that the structure and the content of your thesis develop cohesively together. Structure is dependent upon content. Content is generative of style. At the same time, however, you need to make the moves required of every thesis to the satisfaction of the examiner. Furthermore, you must also observe disciplinary conventions and maintain the integrity of your research data. Thesis style commonly varies slightly throughout the thesis. Often, for example, the introduction is written in fairly easy-to-read prose while sections that deal with theory are denser. The next section discusses some of the ways that the required moves of the thesis may affect style and also structure.

● Contextualizing writing: working with conventions

Most of the time, academic writers use writing conventions without concerning themselves unduly with their purpose or the historical context out of which they arise. Nonetheless, there is a school of thought which argues that academic writing should be looked *at* rather than *through* because its function – communicating research findings – is so significant. To put it another way: it is sometimes important to be reflective about writing so that we can put it to its best use.

Thesis writing, according to Kamler and Thomson (2006), is all-too-often approached as a set of problems to do with grammar and style, and is not considered as a complex work. Accordingly, they regard writing guides for doctoral students as offering a 'one size fits all' mode that is fairly reductive. The basic thesis structure that we discuss in Chapter 1 is a generic form to which these authors take exception. They argue that, because it is pre-determined, it disallows the *specific* argument of the project to provide the overarching structure for the thesis (Kamler and Thomson, 2006, pp. 84–5). We agree, adding that structure choices are often difficult because they affect what the thesis actually becomes in terms of its underpinning values (axiology). The strategy suggestions in this book are not simple recipes you might decide to follow, but are instead a series of perspectives on the potential of your material which are designed to aid decisions.

Furthermore, for many thesis authors word choice, voice and style, and the actual writing of the thesis, create the author's academic position and identity. The phrase *writing up*, as Kamler and Thomson point out, disguises the fact that research findings are produced in the process of writing, and are not simply transmitted (2006, p. 5). Taking their cue from Richardson (1990), these authors maintain that writing *is* research, or at least a part of it, and not a separate activity.

Like these authors, we regard thesis writing as necessarily occurring within institutional expectations and conventions. Kamler and Thomson's book, aimed primarily at supervisors, encourages readers to regard the production of doctoral theses as a process that is situated in broader discursive contexts. It occurs within 'a particular time/place/tradition' (2006, p. 8). Their work is in line with poststructuralist ideas about language, which emphasize that it is less a transparent medium than a concrete or visible 'set of social relations' (Bleich, 2001, p. 119). We highlight throughout the book that thesis writing contextualizes your voice within your discipline's discourse: it is an act of social engagement, a commitment to a community.

For thesis writers, it is important to make considered use of the conventions of thesis writing in order to produce a thesis text appropriate to the context. As Rankin (2001, pp. 67–8) writes:

> Although conventions, like social manners, always evolve for a purpose, once in place they can sometimes calcify and feel more like meaningless rules than useful templates. If we follow these 'rules' without thinking about them, we risk making our writing dull and mechanical. If we understand and use conventions wisely, however, we generally find that they help us to communicate effectively.

Next we briefly look at some of the conventional moves of thesis writing and reflect on their purpose. As Rankin suggests, gaining an understanding of the conventions of disciplinary style and structure can assist a writer in communicating effectively. We consider some of these below.

Moves and styles

To begin with introductions, you could consider how their style contributes to their role in the thesis's social engagement. Why should an introduction be written in a simple prose style, leaving the more complex work for a later point in the thesis? Readers need to be ushered in to any text with decorum. If you were having a dinner party (to use a well-worn metaphor for research writing), you wouldn't hand over the lamb roast the instant someone removed their coat. You would, we hope, first draw them into a warm and inviting room, offer a drink, and gradually move to a light aperitif or entree, before the main event. Readers and diners alike need to be able to build a sense of anticipation and to establish comfort and familiarity. Introductions (as the term indicates) familiarize the entrant with the situation they are in and gradually prepare them for what is to follow.

For the introduction to ease the reader into the text, it needs to be engaging, clear, and convey a sense of moving forward. It could be a point in the text where you outline the reasons why you undertook the research and the choices you have made in conducting it, and so it might have more of your presence in the text. Often the first-person pronoun is used in the introduction, disappearing once theory, method and data are in focus later in the thesis. Ideally, the introduction should also convey your enthusiasm for the project; if there is a point at which you show some passion for what you have done, the introduction is it!

The style will shift throughout the thesis. In a section where you are for the most part discussing other literature, which may or may not be a discrete 'literature review', as we will discuss in Chapter 1, the style of writing might move between a descriptive or summarizing mode to a more analytical and argumentative mode. The writing style might also be quite descriptive when accounting for a method used or *what was done* in the research. Theoretical sections, on the other hand, may produce your most gnarly prose: you may find that you need to grapple most with these parts of the thesis as you try to express complex ideas in an accessible style.

What we are suggesting is that *structure*, the organization of a written text, must work in tandem with considerations of *style* and *voice*, or the mode of writing. This brings us back to disciplinary conventions: as with structure, a thesis writer's voice is produced within a particular set of conventions. Readers in each field come to the text with expectations, and a desire to be greeted in a way that is familiar. Every writer learns to 'speak' in the language of the discipline to communicate with others. Eik-Nes (2008, pp. 185–6) addresses this issue and makes the distinction between 'front stage' writing and 'back stage' writing:

> In writing, we can consider front stage writing as the genres we write for a particular audience. Examples of front stage writing for an engineer would be reports, grant applications, research articles and formal letters. For each of these types of writing there are conventions that must be adhered to, and failure to follow the conventions may result in the reader (audience) refusing to even consider the text...
>
> Back stage writing, on the other hand, is a more private type of text. Examples of back stage writing are diaries, writers' notes to themselves, early drafts of texts that may eventually be public texts. In these back stage texts, writers are not constrained by their readers' demands and expectations.

Eik-Nes suggests that thesis writers can practise the 'front stage' mode in the 'back stage' texts by trying out different voices and working with disciplinary conventions to see what works. It is important that a writer can master the language of their field of research in order to come across as having authority in that discipline.

As we have found in our work with doctoral students, thesis writers don't necessarily gain a broad perspective on the workings and conventions of other fields but usually do have familiarity with their own. If they were to 'cross over', however, and read (or, better, write) in another style, it might throw into relief the conventions of their own. To facilitate this kind of comparison, Madigan *et al.* (1995) compare 25 articles taken from scholarly journals in four different fields: literary criticism, history and two areas of psychology. Their analysis focusses on the use in each field of four stylistic markers: citations, quotations, subheadings and discursive footnotes. As the authors observe, the different uses of these stylistic markers give 'each discipline its own characteristic voice' (1995, pp. 429–30).

We want to draw attention here to *one* of these stylistic markers – the use of subheadings – to demonstrate how a structural move is grounded in disciplinary convention. According to the study by Madigan *et al.*, subheadings are not common in literary criticism and history, but are widely used as a structuring and rhetorical device in psychology and other branches of the sciences. Whereas transitional devices like bridging paragraphs signal what is to come in literary studies or history, in the sciences, subheadings function to announce the next major topic. This reduces the need for authors to make the (more wordy) transitional moves to connect different sections of the text, allowing a written style characterized by brevity (Madigan *et al.*, 1995).

However, when one of us (Frances) wrote her own doctoral thesis in literary studies, she decided to use subheadings. It was not common, as far as she could tell from other theses, but she felt that subheadings would help make connections between different parts of the text. The linear argument and transitional phrasing helped propel the thesis *forward* whereas the subheadings helped the reader to make links *backward* by echoing earlier terms. Although her supervisor was initially sceptical about the use of this device, by the completion of the thesis the supervisor agreed that the subheadings worked well to give shape to the thesis text. Our own survey of students found that they commonly used more subheadings in their thesis than in earlier papers, in line with the different reader requirements of a longer work.

Not only does mastering the conventions of a discipline grant the author a degree of authority, but it can also mean that you are in a better position to subvert them and place your own stamp on your thesis. Poets play with traditional Shakespearean or Petrarchan fourteen-line sonnet forms to make a point: *my* love is different, new, unconventional, and therefore my sonnet reflects that. Shakespeare himself is well-known for having utilized and reworked traditional writing conventions (even inventing new words) and for having adapted the Petrarchan sonnet form for his own ends. A central message of this book is that, if the traditional form doesn't work for the specific content, as Shakespeare found, adapt it.

● Interdisciplinary theses: which conventions?

'What was hard about structuring my thesis was the fact that I don't have one discipline's guidelines to follow and yet my supervisors each have their own ideas of structure based on their disciplinary backgrounds,' reflected one of our graduate student survey participants. If thesis production occurs in particular disciplinary contexts – each of which has its own conventions – the implications are that, for students who cross disciplinary boundaries, there are likely to be some challenges. Textual features that are commonplace in one discipline can mark the author as an 'outsider' in another field.

There are several strategies for interdisciplinary writers grappling with two different sets of conventions. One is to try 'back stage' writing in each style to test which fits best with the research topic. Alternatively, a 'front stage' test is to contribute to a journal that uses the less familiar conventions, thereby really stretching yourself to get to grips with its idiosyncrasies. You can make use of appendices so that material is available for readers who need it, but optional and so not distracting for those who don't.

On the plus side, learning to write in a variety of modes renders writers very flexible. This flexibility enables writers to 'speak' with confidence or authority in a range of written situations and contexts. If you do have to make a choice concerning which set of conventions to follow for structure and style, there are some issues to consider:

● Which conversation are you likely to contribute to? What are the structure and style conventions used by the researchers you most often refer to, reference and read? What are the conventions of the journals you are most likely to be publishing in?

● Which style fits best with the *purpose* of your text, or the nature of the research you have undertaken? It is difficult, to take an obvious example, to undertake textual analysis in American Psychological Association (APA) style or to discuss participant responses in Modern Language Association (MLA) style.
● Which disciplines are your readers or examiners more likely to be from?
● Which structural mode or style do you prefer? Which fits best with *your* preferred style of writing?

Develop some questions of your own that enable you to make decisions on structure, based on what matters most to you about your research project. Consider the deepest level of your research. What *values* drive you? These may be the best drivers of your structural choices.

1 Ordering the Thesis

Deciding on the order in which you will present the entire research project is perhaps the foremost decision you will make about the written thesis. Often at the proposal stage and before much writing or research has been done, a contingent contents page will be drawn up as a way of making the project more concrete and tangible. Thomas and Brubaker (2000) suggest that you consider what you would ask if you 'knew nothing about this topic and ... wanted to know about this research' and then think about the order in which you would like to have your questions answered (p. 245). At the early stages, the structure of the written thesis may blurrily overlap with the expected progression of the research project. To some extent this is entirely appropriate because the end goal of the research project is, for most candidates, the finished thesis. Research design necessarily responds to the requirements of the thesis genre, discipline epistemology (which affects methods) and the candidate's deepening understanding of their material.

We do not intend to downplay the complexity of structuring decision-making, but suggest here that what is generally accepted as the basic model of the thesis gives a useful foundational understanding of the expectations of every thesis. Although the diagrammatic use of mind-maps and models can be helpful for getting your head around all the components of your thesis – and we discuss these below (p. 20) – a basic function of structure is to enable clear demonstration that the academic requirements of every thesis have been fulfilled in yours. First, then, a very basic thesis model operates like a simple recipe, showing the essentials that your thesis is likely to have somewhere. Just as you could adapt the general principles of a recipe by adding or omitting some ingredients, use the basic structure as a pattern that you can adapt in different ways while following the underpinning principles.

🔴 A basic model

The following model is often called 'the basic science structure'. Some arts, humanities and social science theses use this model as well. We suspect that by doing so they are claiming the prestige of scientific research, and making it easy for an examiner to see the 'thesisliness' of the work. They are also following a tried-and-tested formula. If this structure works for you, then you might consider reading no further. However, you may already have been introduced to the science-based structure and found it difficult to apply to your topic, which is why you are now reading this book. The basic model is as follows:

- 🔴 *Introduction*: Why am I doing this research? What is the problem? What is the research question? What are the hypotheses?
- 🔴 *Literature review*: What is already known? Where is the gap I will fill? Which issues, contentions, discourses from the literature are relevant to my research?
- 🔴 *Aims*: What do I hope to find out?
- 🔴 *Methodology*: How will I proceed? What theory will I use? What is my epistemology? What are my methods?
- 🔴 *Results*: What have I found?
- 🔴 *Discussion*: What does it mean?
- 🔴 *Conclusion*: What is my contribution to knowledge?
- 🔴 *Recommendations*

Different advice manuals elaborate this basic model. Glatthorn (1998) points out that 'there are many variations to this basic pattern' and considers that, for example, 'in some dissertations the methodology is so implicit in the nature of the inquiry that ... no separate treatment is needed' (p. 124). Murray (2011, p. 144) suggests using the basic or 'generic' model as the starting point in designing a thesis. Swetnam (2003, p. 44) adds that the introduction will additionally answer: 'Who is likely to be interested in it? What is the possible use of the research? What is the locus and focus?' The basic model will work for some students, but the nature of the particular research project and its significance should always take precedence over the formula: that is the mark of a doctoral thesis.

Thomas and Brubaker (2000, p. 245) suggest a slightly different basic outline that suits a theoretically-based thesis:

Chapter 1   The Nature of the Problem and its Significance
Chapter 2   Theory for Interpreting the Phenomenon that is Studied
Chapter 3   The Research Design for Testing the Theory
Chapter 4   Data Collection
Chapter 5   A Report of the Results
Chapter 6   An Analysis of the Results
Chapter 7   Implications of the Study's Outcomes

What Thomas and Brubaker label 'Chapter 1' might usually be called 'Introduction' or 'Background'; their logical flow forward maps onto the basic model when this change is made. You can see from these variations that there is a standard forward movement from the background, which might include the work already done in the area, the theories used in the context of the discipline's possibilities, through the methods, to what was found (new knowledge or understanding) and what it means, including ideas for future research. The evident, predictable drive forward gives rise to the truism that each doctoral thesis tells a story.

Readers feel more confident when the thesis obligingly follows their narrative expectations. Although many disciplines prefer more individually-designed structures in journal articles and books, it is possible to find theses within these disciplines that adapt the hard sciences' formulaic language around a set structure: introduction, literature review, methodology, results and discussion. Such adaptation is a defence mechanism, given that some of the so-called 'softer disciplines' experienced years of self-justification before being fully accepted as legitimate scholarly disciplines. Are you an innovator who enjoys risky work, blazing out trails, or someone who prefers the safety of staying on the well-trodden path? If you are anxious about your work being accepted, you could consider using some hard science terms, perhaps even as a contingency plan, at the outset, with the intention of replacing these terms with something cognitively more sophisticated during the process of writing the thesis.

Even the most risk-comfortable researcher, however, should also use the basic model as a checklist for the work which needs to be demonstrated in their written thesis. One very obvious consideration is where the literature will be reviewed. Other approaches to the basic model give different understandings of the components of the topic – how they might fit together and what shifts with the various possibilities – and thus help to establish perimeters to the thesis. The order of the moves that the thesis makes should ensure the strongest possible presentation of the research work.

In some disciplines, the basic thesis formulae would look simplistic. However, the work done by these sections of a science thesis will also be done in one way or another by the exegetical thesis. Wisker, giving consideration to arts and humanities theses, proposes that a typical thesis plan is:

> title; abstract; preface/acknowledgements; introduction; literature review/theoretical perspectives chapter; methodology and methods explored and explained, including the design of the study; presentation of findings and results (a separate chapter for scientists only): for social scientists, arts and humanities students, the results, or data, are seen as evidence for the argument, findings and claims based on the research, and they appear in a dialogue with such claims, that is, presentation and discussion of results, analysis, arguments, development of ideas based on results—interpretation of findings; conclusions: both factual (what was found) and conceptual (what does it mean? what does it add to meaning and understanding about the area/field/issues?) appendices/statistical tables and illustrations; bibliography. (Wisker, 2008, pp. 281–2)

Even if you use the basic outline as one to resist and work against, we expect that knowing what it declares to be appropriate will help you to produce a more elaborate artifice.

If the science model looks like a workable one for you, perhaps with some adaptation, then the outline of your thesis structure is in place and you can move to the next level of structuring. Rountree endorses taking the path most usually taken, expanding on the metaphor 'thesis as journey' with a vivid inset story:

As we snaked up Ruapehu [a tall snow-covered New Zealand mountain] the guides gave us nifty tips, one of which
was to plant your boot in someone else's bootprint to avoid
slipping on the glassy virgin snow. It worked. With a thesis too, if you want to cut down on the risk of slipping off
track and losing your way, perhaps permanently, it is safer
to take the well-trod path – to examine other theses, choose
a methodology, structure and style you admire and think
will work, adapting it to suit you and your particular project.
This sounds like dull advice, but doing a thesis at all is ad-
venturous enough. (Rountree and Laing, 1996, pp. vi–vii)

If following a basic generic thesis structure will work for
you, follow the path most commonly taken. Your research
topic should provide some adventure even as you follow the
well-trod path.

⬤ Mind-mapping and modelling the thesis

Some doctoral candidates find visually-conveyed information
especially accessible. You may be familiar with mind-mapping
as a way of getting an overview of all of the potential components of your thesis. To mind-map, one begins with a central
idea which then spreads out with more ideas that emerge from
the central one. More is better. A page covered in radiating
nouns can show the topic's most promising connections. The
strength of mind-mapping is that it side-steps structuring decisions, freeing up the potential issues, themes, topics and backgrounds to speak of their own accord without your authorial
structuring. Mind-mapping allows you to trace through your
material from different directions, opening up some of those
possible parallel universes mentioned in the Preface. It should
also allow you to select which one you will inhabit, and to
move on from the chaotic mind-map to a diagrammatic model.
The mind-map can be activated as a concept map (Novak,
1998), which adds the verb connections between the nouns of
the mind-map. The verbs establish which of the terms *gener-
ate* others, which *restrict* or *compromise* others, and so on: the
verbs begin to make sense of the geography of the map.

The next stage of the process is to start imposing structure onto the mind-map's insights by making a working diagram of the terms that seem most promising. The diagram pattern may begin with nouns that form the topic of the thesis, but the verbs of the concept map should suggest ways of fitting the ideas together. What geometric shape best accommodates your ideas? Dunleavy (2003) recommends graphic devices such as boxes, lines and arrows to help structure the ideas. These may be developed further to give a geometric shape to your work. Often a grid, like the example that we discuss next, works well.

The grid with two options

Once you have a diagram, play with it a little for improvements. Davis and McKay (1996) provide a diagrammatic example that involves reorientation from the model of a grid system. Discussing comparison and contrast, they further observe what they perceive to be the two main options of structure: the topic-by-topic approach and the point-by-point method.

In the topic-by-topic approach, sometimes called the divided approach, each topic is discussed separately. This can be represented as follows:

Topic-by-topic structure:

Topic 1
   Point a
   Point b
   Point c
Topic 2
   Point a
   Point b
   Point c

The second approach is the point-by-point method, sometimes called the alternating method. Here the first point is developed for each topic, then the second point for each topic and so on.

Point-by-point structure:

Point A
   Topic 1
   Topic 2
Point B
   Topic 1
   Topic 2
Point C
   Topic 1
   Topic 2

Davis and McKay (1996, p. 60) point out that neither method is inherently stronger than the other. It is simply a matter of which design works best for your material.

This resonates with us, from our own experience and our work with students, because frequently in the arts, humanities and social sciences there is something of a grid between the material discussed and the themes that emerge from it. For historians, the material may be events, or social groups; for literature students, it may be texts; and works of art or schools for art historians. Susan had the experience of making a change half way through her thesis when she recognized that shifting her design 180 degrees would enable her ideas to come through more clearly.

> I began my doctorate assuming that the structure would be the same as my Master's thesis structure. There I had a lengthy introduction in which I laid out the social issues I was investigating, the discourse I was joining, and the historical framework for my discussion of four New Zealand women novelists writing around the beginning of the twentieth century. Then each author had a chapter in which I pulled all my evidence from their novels, and I had a short conclusion. So for the doctorate on a medieval motif I assumed I would have one chapter for every manuscript or set of stories framed up with a good solid introduction and conclusion. I didn't even think about structure at all.
>
> But about half way through I realized that the themes, social and political issues feeding the transitive movement of the basic story were more interesting than the manuscripts.

These themes and issues were the reason for my thesis, and were what gave it life and zest. So I decided to totally change my thesis by making the chapter headings about the social and political issues and then cut up what I had written and put each text into the chapter's framework which was a discussion of what the stories meant in social and political terms. For two weeks I was tense as I did a massive cut and paste job, ensuring that I didn't lose the vision I had, nor any of the important passages of writing. The process was satisfying; I felt that it gave me a richer and more meaningful thesis.

For Susan, Davis and McKay's 'topics' become 'texts' and their 'points' become 'themes'. The original running order was structured according to the main works under scrutiny:

Introduction
Chapter 1   *Corcha Laidhe*
Chapter 2   *Wife of Bath's Tale*
Chapter 3   *Tale of Florent*
Chapter 4   *Dame Ragnelle*
Chapter 5   Ballard versions
Chapter 6   Arthurian versions
Chapter 7   Spenser's *Fairy Queene*

The revised structure was thematic:

Introduction
Chapter 1   Social critical background
Chapter 2   Meaning of spatial: forest and court
Chapter 3   Hunter hunted and beastly bride
Chapter 4   Meaning of sexual transformation

The themes were the reason for putting this particular set of texts together. However, at the outset they were not as transparently clear to Susan as they became a few years in. Only then could she articulate them. The texts were static; the themes, dynamic. The logical development of the idea at the heart of the thesis was to make the important themes more visible in the title headings and chapter-level structure once the diagram was pivoted. This freed the chapters to be more concrete and work closely with the texts in building that over-arching argument. The thesis argument constituted the structural framework rather than a list of primary sources.

In our experience beginning in the most obvious way – working with data separately and later reconfiguring them into thematic chapters – may leave the thesis more productively open. We suspect that Susan's experience in literature may be shared by others in the arts, humanities and social sciences, and that many thesis writers might find other pertinent substitutes for 'themes' and 'points' (or texts and themes) that make this model particularly useful.

● Broad versus specific fields

Most thesis writers grapple throughout the entire writing process with controlling the structural placement and delimitation of broad background material. All theses contextualize the original contribution within the appropriate academic framework that often includes the history of the research question or problem, the thought and work accomplished to date, and the acknowledgment of a web of theory or philosophy. Each thesis pulls together several contextual webs, and must link each to the main research question, the thesis at the heart of the thesis. The thesis is also a highly defensive genre. Not only are decisions likely to be explained and defended, but the logic of those decisions needs to be clearly evident.

The work of linking background to research topic is important. Glatthorn (1998, pp. 186–8) supplies a list of questions commonly asked by examiners, which include:

- Why did you choose that particular problem? Why did you not study this other problem instead?
- What exactly were you trying to find out? I'm unclear about the meaning of your problem statement.
- You have reviewed the important literature, but I fail to see what use you make of your review. Can you clarify for me what you learned from the review of literature?
- When you reviewed the literature, why did you decide to review that particular area of study?

- Why did you choose that particular method? Why did you not use this other method instead?
- Can you clarify for me how the particular method you chose relates directly to the problem you have chosen to study.
- Can you relate your findings to other important research in the field? In what specific ways do you think you have made a contribution?

These challenging questions could be avoided at the oral examination by ensuring that background history, literature and methodology are clearly linked to the research question in the written thesis. A reader should not be left unsure of why the study was undertaken, what its intention was, why decisions were made and how the original contribution relates to other studies. The ability to link one's own work to the discipline is essential to establish membership of what Becher and Trowler call an 'academic tribe' (Becher and Trowler, 2001), with the doctoral thesis as the rite of passage entry-point. Examiners pay attention, then, to ensuring that the background to the study is represented clearly and accurately. However, firm linkage risks repetition that can become tiresome to the same reader who will object if the linkage is not clear. A balance needs to be maintained.

Much of the background contextualization will be made in the introduction, frame the discussion section, and be knitted together in the conclusion. It is likely, though, that, as the thesis develops and shifts through its moves, contextualization will need to be re-established within the chapters, perhaps with a little more detail than in the introduction. You will need to decide how much belongs properly in the introduction so that the reader is very clear from the outset about the position of the research within its field, and how much should be kept in specific chapters. One way to make the choice is to ask whether a linkage is tying a broad point or a detailed one to the topic. Some will find it helpful to think diagrammatically. If the thesis were to be drawn as an hour glass, with the broad contextualization at the beginning and the end, and the narrow focus on detail in the middle, would this particular linking point best be drawn as a narrow detail or a broad general link?

Shifting within a chapter from specific close-focus material back to broad general principles will feel dislocated and disorienting. If there is an unavoidable reason for this, it is helpful to signal why you are shifting back out to the general. Your argument needs to be kept clear through your steps and stages between specific and broad.

The literature review question

You will need to decide where in the thesis you will show that you have critically reviewed the literature (for literature students, the term 'literature' means 'secondary material') and demonstrated your comprehensive understanding of it. In the basic science model, the literature review is given a separate chapter. Packaging the literature discretely enables an examiner to tick this requirement off the list more easily. It may also be appropriate to use the literature review to identify the gap that your research will occupy, the theoretical framework in which you work, the practical precursors which nestle around your original contribution.

However, by having a separate chapter you risk detachment of the literature from your research. If instead you embed the literature in the thesis as it progresses, it will be apparent that you have discussed only literature which is evidently relevant to your original work. You also give prominence to your own work earlier on, subordinating work that was previous to your ideas and claiming the centre-stage position of the expert from the outset. If you use a referencing system that allows for footnotes, your argument can occupy the space above the floorboards for your argument with a literature review that supports you in the footnotes below your feet. There is something satisfying about compressing the big names in your discipline to prop up your own ideas.

Further, it may be more sophisticated to back-load the literature in what Dunleavy calls the 'opening out' model. Here, a brief review of literature facilitates the set-up, the core of the thesis presents the original work, and an analysis and discussion of the literature occurs at the end of the thesis when its wider implications are explained (Dunleavy, 2003, pp. 59–60).

Dunleavy explains how this avoids the risk of a slow and boring start rehearsing other scholars' work, after which the original work may seem rather less significant (p. 58). We applaud Dunleavy's insistence that a thesis should be interesting right from the beginning – an ideal principle – but appreciate doctoral candidates' concern that even more crucial than the need to be engaging is the need to persuade the examiner that the literature has been adequately reviewed.

For most writers, some of the literature will be discussed at the outset to establish the scope of the thesis, some will be needed in the core chapters, and some may be most relevant towards the end. Some of the foundational, well-known work is likely to be presented as background to the topic; some will be current and vital to specific aspects of the thesis. A literature review remains contingent until the end of the thesis process. Doctoral candidates must write while they are reading at the start of their work, even when they are not sure of the scope of their thesis or the importance of the material they are reading. We cannot over-emphasize the need for a constant relationship between reading and writing. Then, as ideas firm up, the review of literature will probably need refocussing. It is quite usual to work on the literature review towards the end of the process when the chapters are put together in that first whole draft.

A four-way model

Some thesis guide books make use of a four-way model to envision the generic function of the thesis. Defining these components will not enable you to split your thesis tidily into quarters that cover the moves of the quadrants, but it will give you another conceptual model of thinking about your thesis that is likely to help with structural decisions. Phillips and Pugh (2010, pp. 63–7) boil down the basic functions of a thesis to four crucial components:

- background theory;
- focal theory;
- data theory;
- contribution.

The literature review will provide the background theory. Focal theory requires you to explain with specific detail 'precisely what you are researching and why' (Phillips and Pugh, 2010, p. 65). Data theory establishes 'the appropriateness and reliability of your sources,' the identification of how you might do this being one of your 'professional tasks' (p. 66). An explicit, clear description of your contribution – the original knowledge or understanding that the research produces – is the final component.

You might also consider the main task of your thesis in terms of Dunleavy's (2003) proposition that 'in the humanities and social sciences there are only four fundamental ways of handling long, text-based explanations... These organizing patterns are: descriptive; analytic; argumentative; and a matrix pattern, combining elements of any two of the other three approaches' (p. 63). A descriptive thesis may 'follow the pattern of a storyline set by an external work'; or work chronologically; or 'replicate the pattern' of organizations, legislation or regulations and so on (p. 66). An analytic one imposes categories on the found material (p. 70). An argumentative thesis evaluates found material (p. 71). In concluding this proposition, Dunleavy notes, as we do throughout this book, that 'there is never just "one best way" of organizing a long text' and that different principles will tug against each other (p. 75). However, if you feel that your thesis really is primarily descriptive, analytic or argumentative, or especially if you recognize your own as a mix of more than one of these, you could state this in your methodology (or its equivalent) and overtly discuss how this function of your work affects structure.

● Making use of methodology's moves

Although perhaps less so than previously, for many in the arts and humanities, the term 'methodology' is foreign to working practice, and the idea of overtly describing 'methods' is antithetical. Two of us (Susan and Frances) did not really encounter 'methodology' before we had completed doctorates in literature. In that discipline, it would have seemed flat-footed stylistically to baldly declare one's plan in the thesis itself, even if it might be written elsewhere in a personal journal or diary as a guide to action.

Retrospectively, however, the term makes sense of work within our theses that we simply saw as theoretical contextualization. Sometimes the conventions of hard science disciplines are helpful for ensuring that the genre requirements of the thesis are not only met, but are also patently demonstrated to the examiner as having been fulfilled. Thinking about what your methodology would look like if you were obliged to come up with one can give focus. Tony recounts the process during his theology doctorate:

> Around two years into the project and with a first draft of my thesis almost completed, my supervisor was concerned that, as I turned in chapter after chapter, he could find nothing significantly wrong with what I was doing. (With the wisdom of hindsight, I think what he was intuiting was that, while the individual chapters worked in their own right, something about the whole thing was troubling him.) He arranged for an associate (in the field, but at another university) to read the whole of my first draft, and then the three of us met together.
>
> The advice was that the thesis was interesting, well written and up to the standard of scholarship and originality that would be expected. His one main criticism was that the major moves in my thesis appeared to happen in a somewhat ad hoc manner. What he most missed was something like a 'methodology' chapter near the beginning of my thesis, outlining how I was going to go about responding to my research question, and why I would do it in these particular ways.
>
> I knew the moment he said this that he was exactly right. No further explanations were necessary. I went away and wrote a methodology chapter which greatly helped clarify what I had done, and why. Almost inevitably, this required some re-ordering of my material, some was able to be dumped & a little bit more needed to be added in places, so that I actually delivered in the main body of my research what I had promised in the introduction and methodology.

The other, somewhat broader, criticism was that he felt I needed to background the material of others rather more, and foreground my own ideas. This, he said, was a 'confidence thing'. And I found that doing the major revision to my thesis (outlined above) hugely boosted my confidence in what I was trying to achieve and how I would go about it. With, now, a very strong sense of what the real thesis issue was, the insights I had come up with, and the methodology I had employed to connect these two, I was able more easily to let go of the huge comfort blanket of the ideas of others and place my own ideas more centre-stage.

Tony found that the term 'methodology' prompted him to spell out overtly what he was doing in his thesis in the description of its structure. Once he attempted the task, he was able to see what needed shifting around because this was brought to the surface in his articulation. By thinking of how to describe the 'methodology' by which his own insights connected to 'the background material of others' and 'the real thesis issue', Tony probably added a clarity and sense of focus and purpose to what was a fairly complex, multidimensional thesis.

It might seem strange that one word from a different discipline triggered the solution to the problem of what was not quite working, In fact, it is common for some particular shift in perspective, or lens, to allow insight into solving thesis problems. Although the guide-book approach of offering practical advice has been challenged for its apparent failure to recognize the social complexities of the act of writing in an excellent book on doctoral writing (Kamler and Thomson, 2006), we have worked in this volume on the assumption that some seemingly straightforward strategies prompt a change of lens or perspective to enable movement forward. We acknowledge that writing is a complex social act, requiring multiple evaluative criteria to be met, and entailing the deeply personal and thus potentially emotionally challenging construction of identity and negotiation of deeply meaningful values. One response to the challenges is to consider a series of different approaches in the expectation that somewhere amongst them you may find a way to meet all those criteria and feel that the thesis you submit is a fair representation of your data, your field and yourself.

Another of the fairly practical-seeming parts of the thesis which can do a surprising amount of deep-level work is the contents page. Considering how yours will look should be done as an exercise in thinking about how you will present the argument and the story-line of your research with as much clarity and depth as possible.

The contents page and its implications

The contents page lists what is to come in the thesis body, so it is primarily a navigational device. However, it also plots the design of the thesis and enables the reader's cognitive work to begin. A good contents page shows immediately what is important and how the bigger thesis is built from smaller arguments. The relationship between parts and whole is visible and, ideally, persuasive. Contents pages that work well are a pleasure to happen upon.

The language of headings will often signal the epistemology. In our teaching samples, Leonelle Wallace begins her cultural studies thesis (1996) in a fairly standard style with 'Introduction: South Pacific', but her second chapter signals wit, linkage between theory and practice, and the inclusion of popular dialect with 'Too Darn Hot: Sexual Encounter in Hawaii on Cook's third voyage'. The socially predicated word play of the second chapter title suggests that maybe the seemingly innocent and strictly geographical 'South Pacific' of the first chapter has shades of Rodgers and Hammerstein's 1949 musical, in which the geographical setting is heavy-handedly laden with naive, but nonetheless erotic, desire.

Although software will build your contents page for you when you have finished writing, we suggest that you keep a draft of what it might look like as a work-in-progress document that will help you see the development of your argument more clearly. Such a document is an anchor-stone that holds you on track when you become engrossed with detail along the way. A comparison of the contents pages of recent theses in your own discipline will probably give a range of options, from the single heading option of Chapter One, Chapter Two, to the triple- or even quadruple-levelled model, often given numbers: I.iii.a.1.

Dunleavy always recommends using two levels only for fear of creating a confusing 'fruit cocktail' effect, where the parts become indistinguishable (Dunleavy, 2003, p. 70). His advice points to a sound middle path. There is room, however, for individual preference. Any of the contents pages that you find in finished theses must be regarded as 'successful', but you are likely to find that some are more persuasive than others, or look more suitable for your own thesis.

The advantages of simplicity are that a single-tiered system may suffice, and will be easy to build, uncluttered and self-assured. Furthermore, when a thesis is exegetical – building its ideas through the writing process itself – it may be important to the integrity of the enquiry that openness at the outset avoids a prescriptive approach. A single-tier approach enables such openness of enquiry: you are not committed by a pre-designed overview to take the enquiry in any one direction and instead you can be steered by the data themselves. However, a single tier of titling may look a little raw, and fail to take full advantage of the opportunity that greater complexity can reveal immediately to the reader regarding the thesis' sophistication and depth. A single-tier contents page does not give away much about what will be in the thesis. This model is the default option – the plain brown wrapping paper approach to the look of your thesis from the outside.

The advantages of complexity are that you may be able to *think* through the process of constructing the multiple tiers of the contents page and, thereby, get clarity for your ideas as to how they properly fit together, and which ones are more important than others. At one level, liberal subtitling is simply a courtesy to the reader, enabling them to find what interests them quickly. More importantly, though, subtitles give you handles on the progression of your material throughout each chapter, and make revision a little easier because the layout is more evident. Subtitles force you as a writer to ensure that each section is appropriately confined to the topic of the subtitle. In the final stages before submission you could consider whether your readers need all the subtitles that you have used as writing tools, and remove any that seem too low-level. A plan entails thinking through the larger argument and, with this work done, the task of filling in the material underneath each heading and subheading becomes relatively straightforward. Attention to detail ensures that you give yourself a plan and thus a map to follow.

Significantly, the system of subtitling in tiers implies hierarchy. The more complex your design, the more difficult it is to maintain tight control of the hierarchical semiotics of your subtitling. You risk shutting down your options before you have done all of the thinking and writing that might have produced a richer outcome than the initial contents page plan allowed. You must also take responsibility for establishing a more elaborate system and maintaining it with accuracy. This requires more care and time, and in the end may look cluttered, laboured and uninviting.

One workable strategy is to begin with a single-level system and develop it further once the content has fallen into place, keeping an open mind to the possibility of revision. At the beginning of the thesis process, producing a draft of a contents page may be well down the list of things to do. A working draft gives you another way to think about the overall structure of your thesis, however, so that structure – the bones of the thesis compared to the flesh of content – can be developed simultaneously with reading and data gathering.

Compare theses that are available electronically in your discipline to see what the contents pages look like. First look for what is practical: how many chapters there are, whether or not they are of similar lengths and, if not, whether there is a common pattern amongst the theses you check. For example, does the introduction tend to be longer or shorter than the other chapters? Then look for how much the contents page tells about the content. How many layers of subtitling does each have? Do the headings make use of metaphor? How dynamic and explicit are the headings? For example, an introduction could be called 'Introduction' (which conveys no specific meaning at all); 'Introduction: Background to Education in Human Geography' (which conveys the broad context); or 'Education in Human Geography: A Social Constructivist Perspective' (which signals the broad context and the author's theoretical position). An examiner is unlikely to criticize a bland contents page that does not convey the argument or story of your thesis through careful use of language. Ideally, you should strike a balance between something that is so colourful it looks unlike a thesis and something that is empty of meaning, so choose the subtitle levelling and language that best carries the important cognitive drive of your thesis. A reader will subsequently benefit by being able to see from the contents page what the thesis does theoretically and methodologically. The contents page becomes an inviting entry into the thesis.

● Two basic approaches: write first; plan first

This section is a reminder that structuring usually entails a mixture of planning and writing into the topic. Some thesis writers will be able to draft a contents page, work downwards to fill in more subheadings, and finally complete the thesis by fitting their material in between the subheadings. For other students, the processes of thinking and writing are interwoven to the extent that they are virtually the same. Rountree and Laing (1996) suggest that there are two basic approaches to structure. The first is to write first and then highlight the themes that emerge; the second is to get an overall sense of the thesis topic through reading and consideration of data, and write a chapter outline before starting the writing (Rountree and Laing, 1996, pp. 142–4). In part, the approach you use will depend on your discipline and topic, but it probably depends too on your own preferences, your comfort or discomfort with chaos, your eagerness to get going or your desire to wait till you have a good road map. As authors, the three of us found we varied strikingly – but managed to avoid blows – in our personal comfort with planning firmly and fixedly or allowing prose to luxuriate wildly. We also find in our sessions on structure that there are usually students who are adamant that only one of these methods is viable. Yet both methods work well in different circumstances. If you are ever blocked with writing, it can help to move up to the meta-level of planning.

We speculate that the first, rather slower method of working (write first and find the themes), is often the only approach for many students writing exegetical theses. Parry identifies that this is especially the case for humanities students:

In the beginning, and sometimes into the middle stages of candidature, humanities students report that ... the prime concern is to achieve the necessary degree of focus and to develop confidence that the research is headed in the right direction. Here, the stages of starting out and creative development have to take place in tandem because the architecture of the thesis is conceptually constructed ... from the top down. (Parry, 2007, p. 77)

When a thesis is exegetical, how you say things matters very much, and the values inherent in the thesis are constructed through the writing. It would be unduly restrictive to begin with a contents page plan and write into it. We suggest keeping one open as a work in progress that you review regularly and have on hand to discuss with your supervisor, but this may not be anything more binding than a different lens onto your project and a place to develop the lexicon of your headings.

A chapter outline can be a challenge to produce. Some further student thoughts from our survey data on what is difficult about thesis structure were:

- fitting my thesis into a scientific structure when it was exploratory/qualitative;
- being logical;
- being too close to the material;
- piecing together the material as some is chronological and some thematic;
- volume, variety, consistency.

If you write first, you then have the fairly large task of identifying the crucial themes, setting aside what cannot be regarded as central to your thesis (even if it is fascinating, important and valuable) and then finalizing the contents page structure. If you prefer the method of an early outline, you face these challenges at an earlier stage in the process. Even if the contents page must remain hypothetical until most of the thinking and writing is done, efforts to get your head around the project as a whole are generally helpful for enabling writing.

You could consider also the way that people did this work before the benefit of on-screen documents, when writing material was expensive. It is not a new practice for scholars to need to get their heads around larger projects than can be comfortably carried by natural memory. If you feel it is helpful to develop a mental overview, make use of mnemonic theory from past ages. We suggest that the underpinning principles behind memory techniques – make links between things, use vivid imagery that conjures up associated but perhaps mundane facts – are also worth keeping in mind with the writing process.

Mnemonic theory: the architecture of the mind

Mnemonic theory has classical roots and was developed in the context of religiously sponsored education in the Middle Ages. On one hand, mnemonic theory provides a set of exercises to practise in order to develop the memory beyond its inherent capacity; on the other, memory development was considered spiritual in a time when education was under the auspices of the church. Your soul was refined as you expanded the material that you were able to internalize and retain. Yet even for the most secular-minded, classical and medieval ideas about self-construction are applicable to thesis writers who need to declare a subjective position.

The term 'soul' can be translated to 'sense of identity', with all of the axiological complexity this implies, in the terminology of academic criticism (Carter, 2009). Perhaps the most helpful aspect of mnemonic theory is that cognitive retrieval is theorized as vitally important to the inherent identity of the individual. You are the sum of the material that you can control mentally. Thankfully, in the twenty-first century, we do not have to commit large quantities of material to memory, but we should be aware that structuring a thesis is partly about the construction of identity: it matters. Three useful pointers to the thesis writer emerge from mnemonics: the use of vivid, concrete images to conceptualize the abstract; the use of mental architecture to conceive of structure; and, most importantly, recognition that the cognitive structuring process is ontologically significant (Carter, 2009).

There is a concrete spatial aspect to the memory techniques. Cicero in *De Oratore* (55 BC) cites Simonides (c. 556–468 BC) as the first to theorize on memory (and he is also the first recorded professional poet). Simonides was employed to poetically praise a wealthy client at a dinner party, but fell out with his mean-spirited patron and was subsequently called outside. As a result, he escaped an earthquake that killed all the dinner guests, rendering them unrecognizable. Simonides was called in to identify as many of the bodies as he could, and found he could remember them by envisioning again the dinner table of sociable faces and seeking those who sat next to the ones he could remember clearly. Following this experience, he theorized that, in order to remember more than you might naturally, you should mentally construct a specific architectural place in which things to be remembered could be tucked away in sequence, connected one to the next so that they might be retrieved (Yates, 1966, p. 17). Vivid images with some association with the idea to be remembered were then inserted at transition spaces in the building: the corners, doorways and stairs.

At a practical level, the place and image model of early mnemonics offers the architectural metaphor of a building with its entrance way, its progression through rooms and corridors and its signposts that direct. Many theses use an apt epigrammatic quotation at the start of each chapter which performs the job of a mnemonic image, possibly memorable – a small gem that stands out from the background. The individuation that James C. Lockhart (1997) achieves with epigrams at the start of each chapter contributes to the sense of his confident authorial control. His opening thesis chapter, 'Motivation, Research Approach, and Problem Statement', comes under the auspices of Oscar Wilde's: 'It is a pure unadulterated country life. They get up early because they have so much to do and they go to bed early because they have so little to think about' (Lockhart, 1997, p. 1). This chapter opens with a consideration of land-based industries as economic entities, but the quotation obliquely ties economics to the rural versus urban and local versus international dichotomies that underpin his topic. In this PhD in international business, the topic is greatly enriched by his wide-ranging epigrams (the rock group Pink Floyd also make an appearance: the well-known exhortation to eat your meat if you want your pudding), because they make cultural connections and additionally establish the author's wit and expansive possession of how business is enmeshed in social behaviour and cultural values.

The mnemonic model has implications for style. As with architecture, form must follow function, but it may also develop its own unique artistry. The vivid images that mark transition could help to establish the style, conveying cultural and value-laden connections. Although in the linear construction of the written thesis the tour of the imaginary building can be taken in only one direction, the introductory material of the thesis might explain other possible connections between 'rooms'. To sum up, a spatial conceptualization may show how the parts are fitted together to produce a whole that meets the multiple requirements of thesis genre, discipline convention and the establishment of the academic identity that you want to inhabit.

⬤ Mapping thematically

In Chapter 3, we discuss both metaphor and narrative when they are deliberately exploited over the wider thesis for their potential as structural devices. Underpinning both usages are the *themes* that are important to your research. Here we consider some thematic models for organizing your content within the bookends of the introduction and conclusion. It is likely that to some extent your literature review and possibly description of data collection will be chronological, working from the beginning through time to the most recent point. A logical sense of accumulative force is achieved by ordering material from the least to the most important, which may have a sense of working from the external to the internal core. Many studies apply theory to practice and then cycle back to theory again. Old patterns are applied to new material. The general may be used to investigate the specific; previous international study applied to the local. There are many other options, and the ones you choose may be adapted. If you decide that your structure should be organized so that the themes of the thesis govern the systems by which it coheres, one of these may be suitable for your research.

Chronological

The straightforward earliest-to-most-recent ordering has the advantage of simplicity, and is particularly suitable to theses where progression is being studied. It is reasonably likely that even if you have a more complex organization you will work chronologically within some subsections of your work. However, if your thesis content logically fits into an uncomplicated time line, this gives you the equipment to use time as the linking motif. Such linkage will, of course, merely underpin the development of your argument and analyses of what events mean. Davis and McKay observe that: 'The shift from narrating when events occur to arguing that when they occur they produce certain changes is crucial to developing an effective form of analytical writing' (Davis and McKay, 1996, p. 78). They argue that the chronological becomes more meaningful when it is represented as causal: linking the argument development to the time progression is likely to enable the argument to progress logically within a framework constructed of time words.

Least to most important

A sound way to construct an argument is to put forward the second-to-strongest point first, and then steadily work through from weakest to strongest. The advantages of this model is that you interest your audience with something that is reasonably convincing, and then you roll back to the least convincing point, leaving yourself the advantage of gathering momentum as you go. You also finish on the strongest point at your disposal, a powerful rhetorical strategy. For some, instead of generally working chronologically within each section, it is more effective to build an argument based on the strength of each point, and to maintain the sense of momentum forward by working broadly according to this second-to-strongest, then weakest-to-strongest formula. Cohesion can be gained by assuming the linkage of a persuasive dialogic argument.

External to internal

This is a version of least-to-most-important that has a spatial component and a symbolic one. Often, for different reasons, the external is less important than the core. In medieval religious writing, the body is the earthen vessel of the soul; in biological terms it is the internal seed that carries the futurity of the plant. The image of the rose was one that conveyed a sense of each petal following the pattern of the one on its outside, but more perfectly, right through to the tightly curled middle petals at the centre. Philosophically there is a satisfying cultural component to this model, which may allow you to build your content into an envisioned shape that embodies its values. Cohesion is attained through the matching of shape to meaning.

Theory to practice

Many theses begin by establishing theory in the literature review, and apply it to their own case studies, sometimes returning to modify or refine the theory. Grounded theory, in particular, cycles round its processes. In such cases it may be necessary to consider which is most important to the author – the practical application or the development of theory – and to structure accordingly. Often by applying a particular model, such as grounded theory, it is possible to follow specific guidelines that give some direction over the broad outline of the thesis.

Old pattern to new material

A thesis may use a model of enquiry found in previous work and apply it to a new sphere. For example, where a study has found data by surveying a set of participants in one particular location, the same methods might be used to investigate participants in a different place. Sometimes, too, the literature yields possibilities for parts of the data gathering to follow previous models. If you happen to find that this is the case, notice how the model thesis was structured while you are considering how they conducted the research.

General to specific

Literature may show common trends that your thesis investigates in a specific previously unresearched environment. This is the 'macro to micro' model, whereby a small and specific sample is examined to see if what is happening generally applies to this environment or group. It may be that small differences from the general emerge as being the most important features of the area of research studies. In such a case, structure could make use of difference as the organizing principle, working from similarity to difference to put emphasis on the difference found in this study.

Thesis as an hour glass

To some extent, the pattern of general to specific applies to most theses in which the introductory material will survey the literature in order to identify the gap that the thesis will fill. The hour glass is a diagrammatic image of this process: most theses begin broadly as they establish the context of their research question, problem or hypotheses, narrow to their specific topic and work at a close level through the different components before broadening again to contextualize their work within the general field that began the discussion. Critically, once the topic has been focussed down, care should be taken not to spread out to the general again or, if this is necessary, to explain to the reader why the vista has been spread open again.

International to local

A variant is the application of a study founded in international literature that is applied to the local. This is particularly common in New Zealand, where we work, a small country about as far away from almost anywhere else as it is possible to be, whose post-colonial settler identity is constructed around a sense of exile. Research that brings the local into the international discussion steps away from the cultural cringe of parochialism to demand equal significance. We suspect that doctoral candidates from other smaller countries may also be more acutely aware of the staking out of national identity involved in applying an international model locally.

● Ordering the thesis: suggestions for action

First make a mind-map of your thesis by spreading out a good-sized sheet of paper and, beginning at the centre with the central idea, spreading out from there to attach related ideas. Then draw a geometrical model, which might be a triangle, rectangle, or labelled grid, and should include ideas/themes/arguments as well as nouns. Reconfigure this a few times if you are not fully satisfied with your first effort. Keep the model(s) aside for future reference. Put the model that you most favour against the basic structure model. Where in your thesis will be you make each of the moves of the basic science model? Which items in the basic model are most important for your work? You could use a red pen to overwrite the terms of the basic model that are relevant to your diagram, changing the diagram again if this process enables you to see discrepancies and possibilities.

Possibly with your model beside you, overlaid by your thoughts about the functions of the thesis that the basic model provides, begin a draft of a contents page. Look at several recent theses in your own discipline for the options of contents formatting. Develop your own contents page as far as is reasonable and set aside to review in a few months' time. Keep this document alive over the thesis process by reviewing it regularly and changing as your ideas develop. It is something you could show your supervisor to launch a discussion on the development of your ideas.

Move between writing and planning throughout the thesis process. If one becomes difficult, step into the other mode of working. Stay aware of which parts of your writing are broad and general – and, therefore, introductory – and which are specific. Imagine your thesis as a building and consider how the ideas fit together. Think thematically of how your thesis could develop.

● Readerly needs

Some researchers have investigated examiners' comments and questions. Trafford and Leshem (2002) suggest that, rather than being accepted for your findings, you are passed because of your conceptualization of what they mean, and it is your explanation of the process that matters. Johnston (1997, pp. 340–1) reports on positive comments reflecting examiners' attention to structure, such as 'an important study, carefully and thoroughly designed', 'carefully conceptualised' and 'the first chapter provided an advanced organiser for the reader'. Mullins and Kiley (2002, p. 377) found from interviews with 30 examiners that they were aware that the basic science model of structure was not always the most appropriate choice, but none commented on examining anything that differed radically from it.

You need to consider your reader before you submit. Ask yourself what questions would spring to your own mind if you read a single sentence or two describing your thesis topic. If you were to list what you would need to know to be convinced by such a thesis, or would want to know to establish whether or not the research was of interest to you, in what order would you need the information? What would you expect to be told in the first few pages? If the topic obviously has several dimensions in need of some explanation (as in a thesis that examines three different cultures and compares their response to an economic trend), which dimension seems the most foundational to the entire idea? And then what next?

A reader is likely to have some understanding of the background to your thesis topic, but may not have any knowledge at all about some of the details. If you make some interdisciplinary connections, you need to cater for readers from both disciplines, expecting that they will not have a grasp of the other discipline. You will use structure to build a framework to fit your ideas together accessibly for people with a limited understanding of your material, of your theory, of the epistemology behind your methods and of the values that drive the project.

If you feel that there are a couple of options for the order of your material, talk through the benefits and disadvantages of the options, preferably with your supervisor. You may find that this enables you to see more clearly which one is slightly preferable. Then write down your explanation so that it could be included in your introduction as part of the defensive work of the thesis.

2 Emphasis and Proportion

Structuring also results in emphasis. It is common for thesis writers to grow *less* sure of their structuring choices as they understand their data better because they understand the topic's complexity more deeply. They may also feel increasingly committed to the possibly-unexpected significance of what they are finding. Ideas are likely to be entangled like rhizomes, and the implications of their tangle may be meaningful. Carter and Blumenstein (2011), who established a startling negative co-relationship between confidence about structure and time spent on doctorate, conclude that perhaps this is a symptom of increased expertise. The study of 92 students found that about half of the students who gave reasons for changing structure did so because of a shift of focus or emphasis (Carter and Blumenstein, 2011). So you also find yourself feeling less secure about structure the nearer you are to completion; accept that this may be a sign of increased expertise.

At the same time, look at the deeper levels of significance to fine tune and finally choose your structure. If you have experimented with modelling your thesis as a diagram, you are likely to have uncovered various different theses that you might write. Deciding which of your potential topics should be central and which should be peripheral (and maybe those that really ought not to be in the final thesis) involves decision-making about emphasis.

Perfectionists should not let increased understanding act as an obstacle to writing. Some moments of indecision are quite necessary to good writing. When you have successfully completed your thesis and advance towards publication, you are likely to get another opportunity to place emphasis differently, and to produce articles from some of the material that does not survive in your finished thesis. You are becoming an expert on your topic and probably in your field too: you might roam further in this field once you have gone through the process of turning some of the material into a good thesis. Thus, the limitations you face in this task do not apply beyond the examination: any of the material that you exclude from your thesis is sitting fallow and fertile for the future.

The task remains as to how much thesis space should be given to each topic or idea. Readers expect that if something is given more space, it is more significant than material that is given less space. The emphasis given by quantity – more equals more important – is one of the tacit conventions of academic writing. What goes in or out will determine what the thesis actually is; the proportions of included material should secure the development of the argument if the ratio of word count is approximately the same as the ratio of importance. Even if you declare something to be of central importance, if you give it considerably less space than some of the other material, readers will have difficulty feeling that it truly is important.

● Quantity ratios

Doctoral theses are commonly 70,000 to 100,000 words in length (with notable exceptions in some disciplines, such as mathematics, where they are generally much shorter). Overall size defines the scope of the topic: the envisioned project often needs to be down-sized once the reality of the word-count limit is matched against the initial vision. Academic writing is not weighed out and evaluated quantitatively, like a ream of paper or a sack of rice. Examiners will want to see that your thesis is about the right size, not too large and not too small, but they judge it on quality rather than quantity. Nonetheless, as you plan the thesis structure, reassessing the ideas in terms of how many words would probably be needed for each stage of the thesis gives another way of evaluating the ideas themselves and guiding your reader to their worthiness.

Size is defined by thesis genre. If you cannot fit your plan into that word limit, you will need to look critically again at what the thesis actually is, and cut it down to size. Around 80,000 words is a good size for a thesis. With more theses coming through and requiring examination, there is generally less tolerance for an oversized thesis: examiners simply lack the time and stamina to remain fully engaged with a thesis that exceeds the conventional word limit too greatly unless it is spectacularly compelling. Although we acknowledge that it is often not possible, it helps if you can reach this word limit by a straightforward route. Considering size in terms of emphasis throughout the process may help you to find that route while, more importantly, keeping yourself focussed on what aspects of the work make your most significant contribution to new knowledge or understanding. The proportion of sections matters then, not only because it shows to your examiner that you are aware of the thesis genre's moves but because it also signals emphasis.

It is common to assume that, besides the introduction and conclusion, chapters will be approximately the same length. Dunleavy is adamant that all chapters should be of equal size, recommending between 8,000 and 10,000 words, so that there should be about eight chapters, with five of these dealing with the core of the thesis, two acting as the lead-in framework and one as a conclusion (Dunleavy, 2003, pp. 46–52). He considers the option of having variations, such as fifteen chapters and a thesis with three main parts, 'where each part is a set of connected chapters' (p. 48), but rejects this option as likely to cause each chapter to be too fragmented and thin. However, in our survey we looked at examples of successful theses and noted that there were variations. Dunleavy's advice offers a good basic model that is likely to suit many doctoral candidates, but there are other shapes that may be tailor-made to individual theses so that the structure is compatible with the thesis topic.

Dunleavy (2003) has found that 'a recurring problem in most humanities and social science disciplines is that students spend so much time and effort on writing lead-in materials that they create a long, dull, low value sequence of chapters before readers come across anything original' (p. 51). He suggests setting a maximum length for the introductory material to avoid a sluggish start. A key thing to avoid is being 'dull'; an introduction should be stylish and engage appropriately with theory (something that requires considerable work). It is thus a place that benefits from revision and editing. It should be clear and inviting. In fact, the setting out of the project is usually as interesting as the finer detail of the core sections, because the introduction establishes why the research matters. In the process of establishing the context, the introduction usually closes with a brief overview of how the thesis is structured. This is akin to a road map which will be embellished with signpostings throughout the thesis.

The introduction might be where you explain the decision-making logic behind your structure if structure has been difficult in this thesis. In the sciences, it is common to advise students that if there were problems in the empirical research, they should be discussed rather than masked. For all disciplines, this principle of explicitly discussing challenges applies equally to problems with the writing, in keeping with the thesis genre's defensive characteristic. Examiners are likely to be satisfied with an unconventional thesis structure if the choice is explained or theorized by the candidate. Writing a section in which you explain the deepest level of meaning behind your choices and articulating this clearly is of enormous benefit to readers if your structure is unusual.

Another under-discussed feature of structure is that it can be deliberately used to assist the reader with the difficult cognitive task of coming to understand your research and its findings by a few hours' reading rather than by living it for three to four years. Parallelism is a sturdy structural principle, a good default position. To use Davis and McKay's (1996) model (explained in Chapter 1), if you have three topics that you are comparing under points, it helps if they are always in the order of A, then B, and then C and more or less of the same length. Again, Dunleavy (2003) is fairly insistent that sections of the thesis should be consistently the same size and proportion.

Yet rules can be broken when the topic suggests that they ought to be. Should it sometimes be necessary to vary order or size ratio, it is likely to help your reader if you explain why in the introduction to that chapter: 'In this chapter issue X is discussed first and in greater depth because…'. Readers accept quite unusual structures and, indeed, welcome the refreshingly innovative when the logic of difference is patently clear, which often means, overtly explained.

⬤ Levels of depth and voice

Perhaps the most difficult theses to structure are those that have layers of different voices and depths. An example of grappling with complex structural options can be found in the evolutionary process of Jan White's thesis (2007), which argues that the late abstract paintings of New Zealand artist Colin McCahon were not simply landscapes that promoted national identity, but were in fact religiously encoded using typological semiotics. Previous art historians have felt that McCahon moved from his earlier religious themes to landscape paintings that were about national identity, but White shows that the abstract paintings follow his early themes of intercession, mercy and absolution, composed in local settings to imply their relevance to contemporary life in the antipodes and in contemporary semi-abstract style.

Because the typological system has continued through the millennia in the Western tradition, White needed to construct her argument through several chronological periods. She had clear evidence that McCahon knew about typology (the well-thumbed Ruskin in his library and the friends he went to the pub with regularly who wrote on or used typology); that he was a committed Roman Catholic (his letters, his earlier works and late church commissions); and that he engaged with art theory energetically (letters, interviews). This layer concerned his professional life (1930s–1980s). White showed how the theory articulated by both artists and church theologians worked, using examples of paintings from the medieval and Renaissance periods. These used typological symbolism in motifs, colours and shapes. The historical layer therefore spanned medieval, Renaissance, Counter-Reformation and Modern periods, but had two separate strands: typological theory and the examples of how this theory was applied to painting in Western arts and literature. White demonstrated, for instance, how the Renaissance artists and thinkers looked back to Classical Greece and Rome and merged Platonic ideals into religious ideals. This was picked up later by the Romantics of the late eighteenth/ early nineteenth centuries who continued to use typology to convey their culturally-defined spiritual beliefs. They, too, used Classical motifs to reinvent the moral and ethical ideals that were key to the Western cultural paradigm. Later again, the English Victorian Pre-Raphaelites reinvented this tradition using relevant romantic myths with which to discuss traditional Christian morals, ethics and beliefs. This tradition was a critical influence on art in the United States and New Zealand during the Modern period.

White then examined McCahon's international contemporaries to argue that their abstraction was different from his when their religious beliefs were different. Finally, she analyzed several of McCahon's later abstract paintings to show that he used typology as theorized by early authors, summarized by Ruskin (and his contemporaries such as Thomas Carlyle and William Wordsworth), and discussed by many of McCahon's friends and contemporaries, including those in the United States and New Zealand, and clearly demonstrated by early paintings that impressed McCahon. Throughout the thesis White had to distinguish her argument from those of the theorists or art historians whose points made up her thesis. Structuring this thesis was difficult; whether she worked chronologically or thematically, there always seemed to be a compelling reason for doing it the other way.

Through the long process of finding a workable structure, White and her supervisor recognized that several of the rationales for structure were in competition with each other. First, chronological expectations suggested starting with the earlier material and working forward in time. Secondly, because McCahon was central to the topic, as reflected in the title, a discussion of his life should launch the thesis. Thirdly, because the argument was that it was religion, not nationalism, underpinning the mature period of his work, these topics, both with their own theory and discourses, should go first to frame the thesis. Fourthly, the discipline of art history suggested that the artworks that were to be compared to show the connections ought to be first, and central. What finally brought the thesis to closure was cutting back on the breadth of this fascinating topic and eliminating some of the comparisons with earlier use of typology and with modern contemporaries so that one thesis clearly emerged. Most importantly, the story of the thesis process, including the challenges of structure, was clearly articulated by White at the outset. The interconnections between the chapters were explained. White's examiners commented very favourably on her final structure, which had plagued her throughout the writing process.

If you recognize in White's story some aspect of your own thesis, itemize the relevant levels of depth and voice. Do you need all of them, or might you get a more un-contestable thesis argument from a narrower depth of field, with the option of future publications examining the levels that you discard from your doctorate? You probably ought to write a description of your structuring choices and see if your supervisor agrees that it would strengthen the defensive work of the introduction.

⬤ Grammatical emphasis

The English language has its covert conventions, many of which you are likely to follow without having thought about them. We will run through a few that affect structure, since the principles of grammar, which have the effect of priming the reader to interpret content, make a good model for the way that the syntax of structure contributes to overall interpretation.

The first and last places at every level of writing are the most significant. In a simple English sentence, usually the subject of the sentence comes first: 'I am going for lunch' and 'The dog has eaten my sandwich' are examples where 'I' and 'dog' are the subject. This practice fosters expectation that the front end contains important information. The moment I say 'the dog' I have established the agent of my sentence – the subject of the sentence grammatically but also in terms of what it is about. The final place is perhaps important simply because it is the last heard, so is remembered. Joseph M. Williams (1997) notes that, as well as the beginning, 'another important "position" in the psychological geography of a sentence is very close to its end' (p. 146), drawing attention to the final stresses of languages. 'Readers assign special emphasis to the words they hear in their "mind's ear" under this final stress, and what they hear emphasized, they take to be rhetorically significant' (p. 147). Williams puts forward a formula for sentence structure that 'simplicity goes first, complexity ... goes last' (Williams, 1997,

p. 140). His examples show that a sentence with a simple subject followed by a longer, more complex predicate is easier to read than when the subject is long and complex and the simple point concludes the sentence. We suggest that this principle also helps at paragraph level, when the clear topic sentence that opens the idea of the paragraph is relatively short and simple. The evidence, examples and justification that follow can then be more complex in terms of sentence structure and the reader, assured by the clear signpost, is likely to be able to cope with turning them into understanding in their own mind.

At the paragraph level of clear fluent writing, the topic sentence is usually the first one and the final sentence gives a summation of the paragraph and a bridge to the next idea. Both these sentences are key places for conveying the author's thesis development. And although this fact is often given as a mechanical rule – a recipe to be rather thoughtlessly followed – its effectiveness in enabling a reader to comprehend is enormously powerful. In a doctoral thesis, the introduction and conclusion are likely to be the sections that are skimmed by readers trying to ascertain whether or not they need to read the whole thing. (Even if you find yourself short of time for careful proofing and checking at the end of your thesis writing, do not fail to work on the introduction and conclusion.) When an examiner first gets the thesis on their desk they are likely to read the abstract, the contents page, the introduction and conclusion and possibly discussion to get a quick overall impression of the task they have signed up for. These are the crucial places for your best writing.

The same principles apply to the way that structure suggests emphasis: the first and last positions tend to be the most emphatic. Important points should not be found in grammatically subordinate positions, or tucked somewhere within the middle of the paragraph. The introduction and conclusion of each chapter should provide strong bookends, aiding the reader's comprehension by conforming to these implicit conventions. A postmodern thesis may deliberately avoid closure and finish with an open end, but in so doing it places emphasis on its own paradigm. The emphasis principle still operates.

In addition, material in the final place will tend to supplant what came before it. Compare the following:

A   We passed a pond filled with lotus plants in bloom. Then we passed a pond filled with plastic rubbish, oil sludge and old tins.

B   We passed a pond filled with plastic rubbish, oil sludge and old tins. Then we passed a pond filled with lotus plants in bloom.

There is a downturn to A and an uplift to B, although both contain the same weight of negative and positive information. The first example is a tragic model, the second is one of recuperation. In a sequence of facts, the finally-given fact implicitly overrides earlier ones. Similarly, in a series within your thesis, the first and last places of discussion are likely to be the most significant. The strategy of putting what you most endorse last is a good logical principle based on the incremental nature of narrative.

● Emphasis and proportion: suggestions for action

Check that the word space you give to each part of your thesis is appropriate for its significance in contributing to your over-arching thesis argument. If you realize that you have included some material out of interest rather than for its relevance, consider removing it and saving it for publication. The effect of fascinating little snippets of information is that they enliven the thesis, but at the potential cost of making it read like a gossip column rather than a scholarly work. Unless you are sure you know that your examiner will value interest over demonstration of academic scholarship, you should avoid too much detail that is not quite linked to your argument: examiners are evaluating your scholarly ability to be selective.

If your thesis is one with multiple layers of voice, consider which layer will be the lens through which others are viewed. Establish a system by which the dominant layer frames the others. Check that the emphasis points of the first and last places hold content that is highly significant. Check that important points are not buried so as to be easily missed.

● Readerly needs

Your judgment with proportion is crucial for clarity. If you are driving an argument forward, non-essential material is likely to distract. You are speaking to a reader's mind, which is alive and active. Throw it something too interesting to ignore and the reader's thoughts are likely to gallop off in that direction, away from your thread of argument. Stalinist discipline in removing excess is required in order to control your reader's progression. You could read Sword's *The Writer's Diet* and take the associated diagnostic 'Waistline Test' to uncover a bevy of metaphors comparing indulgently inclusive writing to a flabby body, perhaps at risk of a heart attack, in contrast to sleek lean writing (Sword, 2007). Then when you are mourning the loss of a favourite passage of writing, apply the fitness metaphors for encouragement. Carefully storing material that you remove will give you a head start for publication in the future, for those articles that perhaps your quality review system will want to wring from you should you find an academic career.

Examiners' reports typically comment on clarity. Johnston (1997, p. 340) found after looking at 51 examiners' reports that the most common topic was the quality of writing, with comments on both grammar and punctuation deficiencies, 'organisation' and 'a sense of priorities and focus'. She cautions against obfuscation. Mullins and Kiley (2002, p. 379) asked doctoral thesis examiners what they required from candidates and the key terms from the responses were 'design, logic and structure'. They also show examiner descriptors of a good thesis that included 'design – where it all fits together' (p. 379). This leads into the topic of cohesion in the thesis.

3 Cohesion

A thesis is usually written as a series of separate documents. The writer seldom begins at the beginning and works solidly in sequence through to the end over the writing process. It is not surprising, then, that when the chapter documents are assembled into one, additional work is needed to ensure cohesion across the whole entity. In this chapter, we outline some techniques for contributing to cohesion in a thesis text. The first suggestion we make is that you suspend disbelief and think of your thesis as a *story*.

Narrative

A friend of Susan's was indignant:

> Everyone calls Ian Watt the foundational writer on the history of the novel, but in his *Rise of the Novel* there is nothing that was not written before him. All he does is turn the novel into a character and tell its history as a 'bildungsroman' (or story of development). We are meant to be post-modern! How come academics fall for a simple story every time?

The answer to her question is that a simple story structure is powerfully persuasive.

Every thesis tells a story. Those who examine theses concur that there must be a narrative to every thesis (Carter, 2009). Many thesis manuals use the concept of narrative, with advice such as 'Outlining the narrative is for many a vital preliminary step to the writing of the dissertation. Time spent at this stage is well invested...' (Madsen, 1988, p. 72). One of the goals of the thesis writer is to ensure that the reader understands what it is they are writing about. All readers have been raised on stories, so narratives cue the reader as to what should come next. Readers do not usually give much conscious thought to the process as they are led along a narrative line, but the way seems familiar. Safe on the storyline path, the reader can focus on the content.

With academic writing in a postmodern age, it is possible that you will choose to take a less-travelled path. Yet the thesis can be viewed as a simple narrative. Every thesis conveys new and often complex knowledge, and a boringly predicable storyline is likely to aid the reader's comfort. As Pentland (1999) puts it, 'Stories are like ruts in the road that people follow and thereby re-create' (Pentland, 1999, p. 712). The writer who runs along in familiar ruts will appear to be taking the right turns, travelling at an appropriate speed. The reader will be focussed on content rather than form, but they are likely to be humming along through the work in accord because it seems somehow right. For the thesis writer, narrative convention gives cohesion and strengthens structure.

Some graduate students in our survey recognized the importance of narrative. Responses to the question, 'What was hard about structuring your thesis?', included comments on the difficulties of:

- generating a narrative;
- creating the 'storyline' in terms of coherence and flow;
- working out which technique tells the best story;
- the challenge to tell stories that develop theoretical insights and background.

Ann tells the story of how she devised her thesis structure with the need for it to tell a story in mind. Later, when she found her argument actually shifted considerably, the story framework still held strong:

My doctorate tackled the question of *what makes an effective senior executive*. It involved a quantitative study of over 200 senior managers from Australia and New Zealand, in which I explored links between personality, on the one hand, and performance, on the other.

I structured the thesis nine months into the doctorate, one summer evening over a pot of strong coffee. I then spent three years slotting bits and pieces of writing into the structure, as the opportunity arose. The final structure was exactly the same as it was on that evening, and I couldn't imagine it any differently.

In order to reach the point of structure (i.e., in the preceding nine months), I immersed myself in the literature. In my mind, I was on a 'treasure hunt' in which I searched for clues that would form a story about senior executive performance. As I followed clues, I wrote a series of short, personal papers to chart my journey. In those papers, I articulated a research question, and located that question in a number of different literatures. I then developed my research methods, and, finally, documented the 'so what' of my thesis: why it mattered to business, and why it made an original contribution. After writing that last piece, I was ready to develop the official thesis structure. It was then simply a matter of sitting at my desk and nutting it out, which only took a couple of hours.

It wasn't entirely plain sailing, though, at least not in the long term. That evening, I had visualized the hard-bound thesis, complete with my name on the spine, as being an 'argument' from beginning to end. I designed every chapter to have a punch-line, which would contribute one major argument in support of a holistic contention, or so I thought. In developing my contention, I tried to write with just the right balance of authority and self-awareness, and, through that process, I convinced myself that my statistical findings would support the contention. Instead, the findings showed the opposite. Quickly, the thesis morphed into an exploration rather than an argument, I humbly reframed it, and was forced to re-think my convictions.

I'm now about to get my thesis bound, as visualized, and it's a momentous time after a marathon effort. I guess I didn't end up with the contention, in book form, that I'd anticipated. However, each chapter within my thesis tells a story about senior executive performance, and I like to think the story was one that my examiners were able to understand, and one that will help business leaders, even though the story is slightly different to what I had envisaged.

Ann was aware that readers can understand stories, so they are helpful vehicles for conveying your insights. However, it can be difficult to figure out the best way to turn materials that you envision as data into a story. We speculate that this is especially true when strong value systems underpin your work.

Stories have long conveyed social values. Pentland (1999), using narrative for the purpose of building process theory in the field of management, considers sequence of events, focal actors, voice, canonical or evaluative reference and other indicators of context and content to apply narrative principles to business process in a way that makes deep level sense of it. He locates the way that:

> Narratives carry meaning and cultural value because they encode, implicitly or explicitly, standards against which the actions of the characters can be judged. In fairy tales (and their close cousins – text books) the moral is often explicit... But even without any explicit moral, narratives embody a sense of what is right and wrong, appropriate and inappropriate, and so on. (Pentland, 1999, pp. 712–13)

Cultural values underlie the discipline-specific prose of the thesis; they may be able to determine what kind of story you are telling. Indeed, 'the hermeneutical researcher most often interprets and constructs new understandings via narrative exposition' (Parker, 2004, p. 168). Parker suggests narrative possibilities:

> The researcher constructs their narrative around a plot that may represent a romance (a quest towards a desired end result), comedy (evolutionary or revolutionary progress), tragedy (a decline from a previously successful state or satire where events overwhelm the actors). The narrative must offer a coherent account that includes all material relevant to the study's aim, and that presents events and themes in a logical progression, drawing on data which best represents the themes being explicated. (2004, p. 165)

It has been proposed that there are only seven stories in the world and that all fiction retells them, sometimes with a twist (Booker, 2004). Although we think this is an oversimplification, we agree that there are some basic story plots that are deeply engrained and recurrent in cultural practices and other forms of expression.

The thesis is not a work of fiction. Nonetheless, the more removed a thesis is from narrative, the more valuable it is for the author to actively think about the narrative forms that might shape the research so that ideas will be accessible to a reader hardwired to narrative principles. Arguably, as Booker (2004) claims, there are a limited number of basic tales and all stories fall somewhere within this range, either following the model or resisting it in some way. Consider a simplified outline of your thesis at large, perhaps looking again at your diagram and contents page. If your thesis were to be viewed as a story, what kind of story would it be?

We will now outline common forms of tales that are centuries old and common to many cultures. To some extent, each genre has a language of its own. If you recognize that your thesis fits into one or more of these story types, you could use their conventions in the lexicon of headings to pick out the story line that assures and convinces a reader. The next section describes in more detail some core storylines that may be relevant.

Bildungsroman: *a narrative of development and maturation*

The *bildungsroman* follows the main character from birth to maturity, with an emphasis on the development of character, or moral self, on the way. Examples in literature are Goethe's *Wilhelm Meister*, Dickens' *David Copperfield* and Brontë's *Jane Eyre*. This type of story begins with lineage, staking out a genealogical claim to legitimacy, with parentage endowing the hero with certain qualities. The hero may be displaced as a child, separated from parents and security and cast into abjection. The *bildungsroman* considers notable events in infancy, which may be feats performed and/or setbacks or challenges to survival and success; they can also be seen as tests or trials.

Maturation is accomplished only after the hero has survived a challenge. Finally, the main character or hero reaches maturity, secures a place in the world, and produces offspring, who then go in different directions, taking the gene pool to new areas. This is the story that Susan's friend complained underpins *The Rise of the Novel* (Watt, 1987) and thus seduces literary scholars into accepting Watt as a foundational authority. Histories and stories of famous people were often told in this mode: it is a comfortable one for establishing the 'life' story of someone – or of something that is inanimate.

How might this work as the narrative of a thesis? If the thesis is telling a foundational tale, or how something has come about, many things could stand in as the hero in this narrative, from a newly developed variety of grape, to an evolving style of dance. In fact, a recent competition, 'Dance your Ph.D', by inviting students to dramatize their research in a stage performance, draws forth a deliberate choice of genre. We use the competition below for a specific example of Romance, but also suggest that this annual competition is likely to give you other instantly available examples of theses declaring their narrative style (and in fact, dancing it).

Quest: a narrative where the purpose is to find a solution

The hero is given a quest, sometimes as a punishment or as a rite of passage, usually as a legitimizing test that will establish their place within a society. The quest sounds impossible. It may have a formulaic dimension, such as things coming in threes in fairy tales. The quest is likely to be on someone else's behalf, possibly saving something valuable. Unexpected challenges may be added to the expected. The hero may bungle things initially. Almost inevitably, the quest is accomplished, but often the hero and perhaps the world is altered in the process. Things (like innocence, idealism and self-assurance) are lost as well as gained or saved. Typically a quest story shows how an individual gives to their society by exerting personal effort to endorse its value system.

How might a thesis narrative work in quest mode? To some extent, every thesis is a quest in that the researcher is setting out to find something new. However, some focus on a topic which is also a quest of some kind, such as a thesis which aims to bring a resolution to a problem in the world. The path to answers (or 'the' answer) is beset with challenges, and some long-held beliefs may be questioned, while others are upheld or new ones are introduced.

Journey narrative

This is the road version of the quest, and might be a journey away and returning, or simply away to somewhere new where resettlement will occur. This usually involves the discovery of amazing things on the way, but also self-discovery on the part of the traveller. Like the quest, it may involve setbacks and challenges as well as feats performed that show the superiority of the traveller. Journeys may investigate cultural difference between the travellers and the people they meet en route, and this difference may be resolved in a friendship with mutual benefit that strengthens both parties, or it may reinforce cultural difference. Early versions of this type often show how what is alien is accommodated through exchange; often they emerge from borderlands culture and are about borderlands negotiation.

The 'thesis as journey' narrative is commonly employed amongst thesis writers (Brause, 2000) as it lends shape to the research process: although there may be side roads, there will also be a forward trajectory and a point of arrival at the destination.

Tragedy: a narrative in which everyone dies at the end, or the hero and heroine die

The hero is a valued figure with many impressive characteristics, but with a flaw that leaves him vulnerable, like Shakespeare's character Hamlet. Tragic heroes often live in corrupt and unjust societies, with treachery a condition of existence. Although they struggle against corruption, through their flaw they are found to be vulnerable. The ending is death. Frequently there is an apocalyptic sense that this is the death of a whole people, the fictional world, and not just those whose bodies pile up on the stage at the end of the show. While these stories are often precautionary, showing the disaster that human greed and ambition can cause, they can also point to the possibility of new regimes emerging. In *Hamlet*, for example, the pile of bodies at the close of the play signals the arrival of a new order.

In a thesis, the rise and fall of a particular person or order of things (a particular ideology, for example) could be represented as a tragedy from which important lessons can be learned. Or the tragedy may be that no clear solutions to problems can be identified.

Romance narrative

Two young people meet and are attracted to each other. Importantly they are both likable and attractive to the audience, young and fertile. However, there is some impediment to their marriage. There may be more than one set of potential lovers, and a tangle or mix-up of identities involved. Class difference and a particularly difficult parent may be factors. Underpinning the obstacle to marriage are conflicting sets of social values. Usually, conservatism blocks innovation. Finally, the impediment is overcome and marriage is accomplished with the general celebration of all. Society is to continue, thanks to the triumph of love, and the overthrow of conservatism's tyranny.

In thesis terms, the 'marriage' of two things could represent a union, and possibly new birth, achieved after overcoming obstacles. For example, Joel Miller, the 2011 winner of the 'Dance your Ph.D' contest, utilized a romance narrative to explain his research in biomedical engineering, as you can see from the title of his dance presentation: 'Microstructure-Property relationships in Ti2448 components produced by Selective Laser Melting: A Love Story' (Dance your Ph.D, 2011). Critical theorist Belsey (1994) points out that romance is a reassuring narrative form, and that in broad terms the motivation of desire and pursuit of wholeness that romance represents is a dominant narrative in Western culture, reiterated in many forms.

Loss and recuperation narratives

Something valuable is described to show its preciousness, which will be recognizable to the audience, and then it is tragically lost. It seems impossible for it to be regained. There may be several attempts that fail, drawing out the pathos of the situation. Eventually, the right combination of quester, fate and season allows the miraculous to occur and the lost thing is recuperated. Again, this story type has optimism in the face of loss.

For a researcher, the loss and recuperation narrative may work for a thesis which describes the loss and discovery of artefacts, to take a literal angle, or for a less tangible precious 'thing' (a nation's prosperity, a cure for a disease). The hero could be someone else whose work or discovery is described – or it could be the thesis writer themselves.

Overcoming the monster

A monster is threatening a whole people, and cannot be stopped in the carnage it wreaks. It may be a historic pest or something new. It may be fantastical and will probably, almost unavoidably, be symbolic of evil, alterity and death. A hero decides to confront it, generally with the blessing of elders, and with some ceremony. The hero succeeds and the monster is banished, usually killed. The hero may be killed too or this episode may be part of the narrative of maturation, or even romance.

In research terms, there are many potential 'monsters'! As with the loss and recuperation narrative, figuring a research problem as a monster to be overcome can offer an effective narrative form for the thesis.

Consider whether your thesis has the potential to be more than one of these story types. Always bear in mind that structure and order affects meaning, and so too does the narrative conventions that your thesis employs.

Narrative conventions

To some extent, narrative conventions map on to disciplines, as we found, to our surprise and interest, from our survey of 92 doctoral students. For example, education and business theses tend to tell romances and to a lesser extent, tragedies; arts and humanities favour quests (Carter and Blumenstein, 2011).

Some material has the capacity to be told as a tragedy or as a romance, or a recuperation story. When there is an option as to the ordering of material, one consideration is whether you prefer to finish positively (opening up possibilities) or negatively (the outcome is 'no solution'). You could consider where you want the thesis to take you in future research or employment, and what your hopes would be for pursuing further research on the topic.

Recognizing which kind of story best conveys the direction of your thesis, and consciously using the language and formula of that particular type, can perform multiple tasks. Your reader will feel confident that the text is progressing in the right way because it is familiar at a basic (non-academic) level. You will get cohesion to the framework of the thesis by exploiting narrative convention throughout it. Consciously selecting the story type will reinforce the axiology that you want to sit behind your study. Are you conveying an optimistic message, or a cautious one, or are you endorsing new generational impulses while rebuffing the conservative? The bottom line is that your examiner must be satisfied that your thesis has a logical progression, developing an argument as the academic equivalent of a plot and avoiding the sense that you are amassing facts without linking them into meaning-making. We focus on meaning-making and axiology as means to ensuring cohesion: the deeper levels of the work can be criteria for selecting the strategies that will ensure that your thesis has cohesion.

Metaphor for structure

Like narrative, metaphor can also be used as a structural device. In the following story, Frances outlines how a metaphor that enabled her to conceptualize the thesis as a single entity *also* provided her with a means of ordering material coherently.

The central metaphor at work in my English literature thesis on the fiction of A.S. Byatt was originally the double helix, used to introduce the themes of the thesis. As the abstract to the thesis describes, it is an exploration of Byatt's engagement with 'a persistent "thread of two" in Western discourse' (Kelly, 2002, p. ii): man/woman, world/word, past/present, self/other. My interest in the dual focus of these texts is made apparent in the chapter headings and subtitles: each points to the interplay between 'two things' in Byatt's fiction and establishes this dominant metaphor throughout the text. In my mind, I very clearly saw this interaction of 'two things' in terms of the double helix spiral. I remember very clearly having an 'a-ha!' moment when I realized that the central argument of my thesis and its overall structure could be encapsulated in the metaphor of the double helix. I remember just as clearly experiencing the feeling that I would have to revise it.

Despite my best efforts, the neatly coiling strands of two became knotty and entangled with other threads. For a while I carried around the image of the medusa-headed starfish, after I had seen one in the natural history section of the Auckland Museum. In some ways, *this* metaphor for the thesis was also appropriate. The thesis includes an analysis of one character's attempt to study the reproductive organs of sea creatures, 'various Hydras and plumed worms that could be got to bud new heads and segments'; each time the amateur naturalist slices a tentacle off the hydra a 'new creature' forms (Byatt, 1990, pp. 248–9). This image of Byatt's naturalist, itself a metaphor for the way arguments can spawn, is possibly the reason for my most vivid thesis dream in which the thesis was figured as 'born' (childbirth is a well-worn metaphor for thesis production), only it was not one child, but two, that I gave birth to, one of whom was two-headed.

Fortunately, the image of the knot (also courtesy of Byatt) brought a kind of unity to the diversity of strands explored by the thesis. As a working metaphor, the knot enabled me to imagine or visualize the thesis as a single entity, comprised of a number of different double-helical strands, which was extremely helpful during the protracted writing process. As a working metaphor, the knot comprised of helical strands enabled me to *imagine* or *visualize* the thesis as a single entity, albeit one characterized by a degree of unruliness or knottiness. The metaphor of the double helix also allowed me to set two things alongside each other, without subsuming one to the other. It allowed me to retain, and not try to resolve, contradictions implied by the combination of opposites (past/present, life/death).

For some writers, metaphor is used to underscore a central finding. Ian's story shows how historical case studies (derived from separate archival repositories) were melded into a thesis structure once the overarching purpose of the thesis had been stumbled upon. The case studies became the chapters. The 'mind-mapping' exercise was an instantaneous 'seeing the light' moment preserved on the back of an envelope. With hindsight, Ian adopted Davis and McKay's (1996) Point A, Topic 1, Topic 2 model.

I only had one 'a ha' moment during the doctorate, but it turned out to be a very important one in terms of structuring the thesis. My thesis research topic was the teenage or 'youth market' in America during the affluent post-war years of the 1950s and 1960s. One day, about 18 months into the research, I read an article in a business magazine from 1964 (in historian's terms a 'primary' document) in which an economist proclaimed that the 'baby boom' generation of American teenagers were now 'ripe for harvest'. That's my thesis title I thought. At this point I had collected data from several archives which meant, in effect, I had several case studies in search of a framework.

Once I had my thesis title in mind I was able to scribble down my chapter headings on the back of an envelope to provide the scaffolding. I knew I would need a literature review of some kind and decided to integrate this into my introduction that would set the scene and give the reader a sense of historic backdrop, the scholarly debates about the historic roots of consumerism and existing studies on marketing to teenagers, a route map for the thesis reader (providing a rationale for which case study came in which order) and, finally, my theoretical approach to understanding historical documents.

The body of the thesis then fell into place. The first section explored the post-war development of youth marketing as a specialist business enterprise. The middle core looked at youth marketing from three perspectives: how a broadcasting company attempted to develop radio and TV programmes that would attract young viewers and listeners and in turn attract advertisers; how a major advertising agency created campaigns for their clients directly pitched at young consumers; and then how government agencies used public-service advertising to promote healthy living to teenagers. This middle core was the case studies that had already been researched. The final part of the thesis core looked at the debate during the 1950s and 1960s over the alleged harmful impact of commercialising childhood and adolescence. My title 'ripe for harvest' was given a question mark allowing for some 'yes' or 'no' conclusions to the thesis. Just because an economist thought youngsters were about to be commercially exploited does not mean they necessarily were.

I converted my brainstorm scribbles into a tidy typed Word document as a mock thesis content page and nervously handed it to my supervisor as the main agenda item for one of our regular supervision meetings. With a few judicious suggestions for making it 'stick' and clear advice on the purpose of the literature review within the introduction she and I had an agreed thesis structure.

My 'a ha' moment got me out of jail so to speak. Without the title as an over-arching concept my thesis might have struggled to have any cohesion. The one thing I should have done was read a few doctoral theses to get a feel for how they should be (or could be) structured. It amazes me now to realize I spent 18 months doing extensive secondary and primary archival research for my doctorate without really knowing how the thesis was going to be structured.

Ian was also a secondary advisor for Helen Laurenson's Master's thesis 'Going up? Going down! The rise and fall of Auckland department stores 1920-1960' (Laurenson, 2003) which uses the metaphor of the department store building itself, with different floors devoted to different kinds of products, as a structural device. It is clear to see in this example the way in which the tenor and vehicle are related; to put it another way, the *form* and *content* of the thesis are aligned through the structural metaphor of the department store.

In Susan's survey of groups of thesis writers, she asked if they use metaphors to talk (or think) about their structure and, if so, which metaphors they use. Twenty-one of 85 responded that they did. This text cloud represents the proportion of mentions a particular metaphorical image received.

alchemy alignment architecture **art branches** brick **building** bus changes **circles** community **concentric** criss cross cubist entire foundation interweaving **journey** knitting lop-sided **map** mind modern moment moving narrative national opera organizing outwards pathways personal photomontage political pyramid quest rigid social spiritual springs **story** strong **structure** sword symphony **think** tip tree yes

Survey participants identified a number of journey-related metaphors, like the pathway or quest, and also spatial metaphors. Other thesis writers have used travel, pathways and journeys, together with spatial metaphors of maps and boundaries, as structural devices.

In the thesis 'Learning to Cross Borders' Francis Collins employs an extended metaphor of travel, using images of crossings, bridges and borders to structure a geography thesis on 'emergent transnational mobility' (Collins, 2006, p. ii). As this short excerpt from the table of contents indicates, the chapter titles are a balance of key research terms, metaphors that relate to travel and mobility, and generic descriptors of content:

Chapter One: First Steps
    Borders, Bordering and Border Crossing
    South Korea and International Education
    Urban Experience in South Korea and Auckland
    Research Participants, Objectives and Approaches
    Organisation of the Thesis

Similarly, in a thesis in literary studies, Sean Sturm (2008) employs the language of travel, geography and nomadism throughout. The author whose work is being analyzed, George Chamier, is termed an 'Epicurean' and an 'unsettled settler' whose mobility is a central thread of the thesis argument. Chamier's travel destinations provide the overall structure for the thesis, as you can see in the excerpt from the contents page:

I   Europe (1912–15; 1842–59)
　　1   England: Full Circle to the Centre (1912–15)
　　Detour 1: Chamier the Epicurean 1 – a Critical Position
　　Detour 2: Chamier – Life and Works
　　2   England: Home? (1842–44)
　　3   Europe: An Intellectual Home (1844–59)
II   New Zealand (1859–69)
　　1   Out to New Zealand (1859)
　　2   The Cadet (1860–64)
　　Juncture 1: *Philosopher Dick*: Raleigh, Unsettler and
　　Unsettled Settler
　　3   The Road Surveyor (1864–66)
　　Juncture 2: *A South-Sea Siren*: Raleigh, Lover or
　　Truth-Lover
　　4   The Assistant Surveyor (1866–69)
III Australia (1869–1908)
　　1   Adventure (1869–71)
　　2   Melbourne (1871–77)
　　Juncture 3: *The Story of a Successful Man*: Tim's Story,
　　the Story of an Unsettled Settler
　　3   Adelaide (1877–90)
　　4   Sydney (1890–1908)
IV   China and England 1908–15
　　1   China (1908–12)
　　Detour 3: Chamier the Epicurean 2 – a Final
　　Philosophy

Sturm's thesis also employs cartographical representations and charts depicting the movement and trajectories of characters in the novels to visually demonstrate their 'unsettledness'.

For these two thesis writers, the metaphors of journey and travel provide structural scaffolding which relates to the thesis content. For others, including some of those surveyed, the journey metaphor represents their own thesis-writing experience. Personal metaphors for thesis writing, such as the journey (Brause, 2000), are a powerful means of describing the process of conducting research and can be usefully harnessed in the ordering of thesis material. If a metaphor has individual meaning and significance *and* can be utilized in shaping the thesis text, employing it is a way of bringing something of the self, or of the thesis writer's values, into the text, which for some thesis writers is a vital element of writing.

Cultural metaphors

The use of cultural concepts as a methodology or framework demonstrates the power of metaphor to provide structure at an ontological level. We have found that cultural frameworks are at work in theses by Māori (the indigenous people of New Zealand) and Pasifika (Pacific Island) researchers, but could likewise inspire any thesis writer whose cultural background motivates or informs their research.

The examples we now briefly discuss bridge the gap between specific cultural beliefs, or frameworks, and academic conventions. Cultural metaphors, like others, give the mechanics for cohesion, but, more importantly, give a strategy for building a structure that embodies deep-level values.

In the thesis 'Me he korokoro kāmako ['With the throat of a bellbird']: A Māori Aesthetic in Māori Writing in English' by Jon Battista (2004), the author uses the concept of whakapapa (which in English refers to both 'family' and 'genealogy') as a theoretical framework *and* a structuring device. According to Battista's abstract, the thesis proposes 'a definition of a Māori aesthetic grounded in the principle of whakapapa'. As she goes on to state, whakapapa is 'the central motif and methodology in the thesis' *and* it provides a structural metaphor. 'The *structure* of this thesis itself deploys the idea of whakapapa as an organizing principle' (Battista, 2004, p. 5). The thesis has two sections: one refers to 'parents' and the other to 'children':

> The main body of the thesis is divided, simply, into two Parts, each consisting of six chapters, and the relationship of these two Parts is itself, also, intended to exemplify a core principle of whakapapa. The first Part examines texts by two major adult authors, one female and the other male, Patricia Grace and Witi Ihimaera. The second offers a detailed analysis of contemporary Māori literature for children. (Battista, 2004, p. 6)

There is a related metaphor at work in the thesis structure: the waka (or canoe). Battista (2004, pp. 6–7) outlines how the two metaphors really work together to underscore the centrality of whakapapa as a concept and structural device:

> This main body of the thesis is framed by a Prologue (a discussion of Jacqueline Sturm's poem, 'E Waka') and an Epilogue (a discussion of Robert Sullivan's epic sequence, *Star Waka*). These brief sections are designed to ensure the association of whakapapa on several levels. The first level allows metaphoric recourse to the waka as a significant symbol of identity – all Māori have lineal ties with the paramount chiefs of the great waka. Furthermore, irrespective of the colonial process and ongoing interventions, waka are the bearers of, and the visual reminders of, a culturally exclusive people and body of knowledge. Jacqueline Sturm's poem as the tauihu, or prow, of the thesis acknowledges her as a forerunner in the submission and acceptance of work for publication. Robert Sullivan's writing a generation later forms the taurapa, or stern. Together with all the other analyses of the texts I have selected, they represent the vehicle by which a Māori aesthetic of writing is substantiated.

Shaping the thesis through culturally specific metaphor enables the writer to inhabit multiple positions as an academic and community leader. The values of the community are emphasized and privileged when they drive the thesis structure. Battista's thesis is an example of this, with indigenous values overlapping with academic ones, which are expressed through a culturally specific lexicon and framework.

Cook Islander, Teremoana Maua-Hodges, offers the tivaevae model as a useful framework for the research thesis (Maua-Hodges, 2000). Tivaevae are the beautiful, large appliquéd bedspreads traditionally made by collectives of women as gifts for special occasions. Maua-Hodges' tivaevae model is another metaphor for research in which different materials from different sources are stitched together into a new larger pattern. Again, it is not new to note that the thesis is 'woven' or 'stitched' in the sense that it is always multi-voiced, built on the research literature, and has supervisors and advisors contributing. The tivaevae tradition of communal creation gives a cultural metaphor that expresses this, making the comparison between the academic and Pasifika communities concrete, visual and vivid.

Behind these methods is the belief that, although academic epistemologies must be considered, so must the deeper-level value that underpins much research. Nabobo declares that: 'Knowledge is connected to the worldview of a people. Epistemological assumptions are, in my view, derived largely from the way a group of people see their world' (Nabobo, 2003, p. 88). Stokes (1985, p. 19) takes the view that 'the traditional detached academic stance of the universities is not only inadequate, but in many situations irrelevant... What needs to be explored now are ways in which other cultural frameworks can be admitted and given appropriate status in research methodologies'.

Having considered the underlying cohesion that can be achieved by deep level, axiological models of narrative and metaphor, with cultural metaphors as examples of well theorized practice, we turn to the language struts and stays that hold the structure firmly together.

Joinery: bringing the parts together

Once you put your chapters together and get your first full draft, you have reached a significant milestone that deserves celebration. This enables you to very clearly see your thesis as a single whole entity. And now a new set of tasks confronts you: smoothing the junctions, ensuring that the texture and tension of the writing is consistent (unless there is a good reason for it not to be) and tying the parts into a whole. The tension (to borrow a knitting term) may have altered as your writing developed over the several years of the doctorate, so that you may need to tighten or loosen up sections that were written early on. The work may need editing so that voice is consistent. It is common to summarize each chapter briefly on concluding it, and to ensure that the next links logically so that the reader can see how it continues the story line. Once the thesis is together as a whole, you may feel that this work is heavy-handed, and cut back some of the linkage, or it may be that some of the junctions are abrupt and bridging work needs to be installed.

The final stage of the thesis is also the time when the structure of the overall thesis becomes more baldly apparent. Approaching submission often creates tension, and frequently candidates feel anxious about earlier structuring decisions. At this stage we suggest that you work closely with your supervisor and any other advisors on hand to get help with judgment. Although you may attend to ensuring good joinery rather mechanically, the effect works at a deeper level to demonstrate that the thesis – its impetus, ideas and analysis – is fully integrated. In advising on the discussion section of the thesis, White (2011, p. 302) notes that referring back to earlier chapters helps to 'place the findings in context and show how the theoretic perspective applied provided particular and valuable insights.' Examiners respond well to a demonstration that you are in control of the written thesis as a whole entity; joinery enables you to do this clearly, as you 'top and tail' chapters, and make the linkages that secure your overall thesis. Other readers looking for what your work offers to their own will also appreciate you actually showing how the methods, literature, and theory work together to make meaning of your results.

It is likely that a major revision of your thesis might give you a more sophisticated or creative thesis; if you do not need to do this, however, simply tidy it up and hand it in. It is not uncommon to lose confidence in the final stages of writing a thesis and you should get a second and perhaps third diagnosis if you feel you need to begin again and do a huge amount of work before submission. Time should be a significant factor when you consider what changes need to be made: there will always be improvements that could be made, but you should do as few of these as you can and submit the thesis. Submission is likely to be the most immediate concern, but the thesis is just one product of all your thought and work. You yourself as a researcher and your future publication are others.

You are likely to need some work on your thesis to provide the guidance and assurance that keeps readers feeling they are in good hands. As Manalo and Trafford (2004, p. 93) declare: 'Your thesis is not a mystery novel'. You will want a sense of progression, and may decide to reserve some findings until towards the end of your thesis, but nonetheless the reader will want to be guided as to where you are leading them. Most readers will happily follow you anywhere as long as you tell them in advance where they will be heading. Here are some pointers for the signposting that is vital for flow and cohesion.

A map

We suggest that the overview map that is usually at the end of the introduction is strongest when it explains the argument's movement and development by describing what is in the chapters. Readers are reassured by knowing what they are entering. A strong overview map will also establish why the thesis flows as it does:

> Chapter one reviews literature to date, using past research to build a methodological platform for this study. Chapter two adds to this an explanation of two theoretical models adapted sequentially to... Chapter three demonstrates the advantages of this combination with five case studies.

Once the reader has the overview clearly explained, along with the reasons for structure, joinery linking the sections will assist them with road maps throughout the thesis assuring them of where they are and where they are headed.

Subtitling

Some graduate students use subtitles throughout the writing process because such usage is consistent with their discipline's norms. Those disciplines that do not usually use a great deal of signposting expect more subtitles in research theses than is common in undergraduate assignments. Data from student surveys (Carter and Blumenstein, 2011) showed that an overwhelming majority of students used subtitles (96.1%) and most (89%) have indicated that the frequency of using subtitles in their doctorate had increased or would increase compared to subtitle frequency in their undergraduate writing. Frances' story (pp. 63–4) also indicates the role that subtitles can have in contributing to the structural cohesion of the thesis, in this instance through an extended metaphor. Thesis length justifies signalling and signposting for direction.

Your subtitling system should make sense of your structuring choices. You might begin in this task as Moore (2000, p. 81) suggests: 'Think about levels within the structure. Some concepts are of equal weight or importance; some are subordinate to others. Reflect these relationships in your structure.' This is sound advice, but some authors may have difficulty deciding where to put emphasis, and which of their concepts should be subordinated, which elevated to top rank. If this is the case, inserting subtitles with (only) the relevant material under them helps to make progress.

All the material on one topic should be kept together for the purpose of clarity. If lack of clarity is a difficulty, installing subtitles, ensuring that only topic-specific material is under them, and then ordering them logically will usually resolve the problem. Sequencing of the sections is likely to be more obvious once the segmentation has been effected. Subtitles provide convenient little handles for the cutting and pasting job if the sequence is not quite right. Your thought on the axiology inherent in storyline and metaphor should help you to recognize how the subtitled parts best fit together. This may be the point where you can see that one section is longer than its contribution to the thesis is worth, or that something significant is discussed in fragmented pieces that might be best put together.

We suggest that you aim to make subtitles as useful as possible by ensuring that they contain your ideas, the spark, rather than more inert material such as facts. The process of writing a thesis takes facts and renders them dynamic in meaning, something larger than their sum. If you could title a section 'The Romantics' which is large and vague, you could ask yourself why you are introducing the Romantics at this point and make the answer your subtitle: 'Nature made divine: The Romantics' or 'Daffodils and cocaine: The Romantics reflect on reality' or 'Romanticism's pre-conceptualizing of reality TV' depending on your main point about this group of writers. For many disciplines, the more concrete, specific and lively your subtitles, the more helpful and enhancing they will be.

Rankin points out that in addition to useful subtitles, you can repeat language clusters in what she calls 'echo links' to show that themes are consistently woven through the thesis (Rankin, 2001, p.30). 'Sometimes the signposts are fairly obvious, as in chapter titles, numbered and titled scenarios... Other signposts, sometimes called echo links, are less obvious because they are embedded in the language.' Simply using the same terms, sometimes phrases, or reiterating metaphors throughout the thesis will provide weft links through the text.

Once the final draft is fused together as one document, it is possible to see repeats throughout the thesis more clearly. To avoid repeats of explanatory material, hook sections with directives such as 'explained further in Chapter 5'; 'described briefly above in Chapter 2'. This linking complements the use of 'echo link' phrases that carry idea strands throughout the thesis. White (2011, p. 132) uses the terms 'preview, overview and recall' for joinery sentences:

> Previews anticipate what is to follow later in the thesis or, as in the following from a chapter introduction, later in the same chapter: The following analysis is represented in two stages. *In the first the current perspectives on... are evaluated. The second is a critical evaluation of* ... Overviews may look in both directions: *In this chapter the reason for ... has been discussed. In the next section this discussion will be elaborated by...* Recalls look back on the earlier stage of the text: *As described in the introduction...* (Emphasis in original)

Nonetheless, White cautions that such sentences should be used with caution. We agree that a balance must be found between providing the comfort of a clear framework of the thesis' direction (which aids an examiner's evaluation of your overall control) and avoiding boring the reader through too much pre-emption and repetition. Those echo links should not develop a hollow ring.

Explaining structure in the introduction

Examiners read with a sense of duty: the role obliges them to question your choices. You are likely to need to add more explanation of your structure with the vision enabled by the first full draft. Tony's story in Chapter 1 (pp. 29–30), recounting his writing up of a methodology section, tells of this process: having to explain what he was doing in his thesis enabled him to see what was not progressing logically, and to install more cohesion through shifting things around and removing some of them.

The more unusual and creative the structure, the more in-depth this defensive explanation should be so that there is no risk that an examiner might fail to see the principles at work in the structure. In our experience, structure can be a highly innovative aspect of the thesis, but when this is the case, it needs to be theorized and defended early on so that examiners feel choices were sound academic ones, in keeping with the epistemology of the discipline(s).

A final task will be ensuring that the prose itself emphasizes the contribution to research. The conclusion should have an emphasis to it that removes the 'so what?' from the reader's mind. Thinking of the introduction and conclusion as bookends may help to ensure that the originality of the study is underscored in both these significant places. Ensure that if the topic shifted slightly over the duration of the doctorate, the conclusion does in fact anchor all of the ideas that initiated the written thesis in the introduction. Read the two sections together and ensure narrative integrity.

Readerly needs

The shift from author-perspective (what do I need to say?) to reader-perspective (what is it my reader will understand from this?) is not always easy, particularly after several years of engagement with the writing process. Yet your ability to make this shift and provide support for your reader is likely to make the examination process smoother. It has the added benefit of making your work more accessible to a wider range of readers once it is completed. The ability to step back and read your own work as a reader who is not familiar with your topic would is an asset to add to those that you have already acquired during your graduate studies. Thomas and Brubaker (2000, p. 245) suggest that you consider what you would ask if you 'knew nothing about this topic and ... wanted to know about this research' and then think about the order in which you would like to have your questions answered.

Imagining an audience *is* an important element of writing. Give your writing to others to read on a regular basis: your supervisors, members of a writing group, other doctoral students or colleagues in your discipline. Get used to writing for an audience that is scholarly, but not too intimidating. Consider what it is that your audience *knows*. Ask yourself:

- Who will be reading what you write? Will they have an inherent interest in and extensive knowledge of it?
- Will the reader(s) be able to follow your argument? Do you need to include 'signposts' along the way? Is it logical? Can the reader(s) make the connections?

These questions open up the final stages of the thesis process in which you need to swing your head from your authorial perspective to that of the reader, ensuring that structure enables readerly comfort as well as being true to your topic. We suspect that it is only once you have a complete draft together that you will be able to truly focus on the reader's needs of the whole thesis.

Conclusion

A thesis is a curious, multi-tasking act of communication. Firstly, it is a tough old nut with a rich kernel: new knowledge or understanding. For survival, that kernel must be accessible; clarity is crucial. Secondly, the thesis is an entry-point to a research profession. It must demonstrate its author's command of the practices and languages of the field of research: the thesis represents a ritualistic demonstration of maturity within a specific community. Thirdly, the thesis is an act of self-fashioning. Its theoretical positioning and textual voice creates the academic persona that its author is likely to inhabit for some time. To some extent, you create yourself in writing a thesis, and, as a live author creating the textual presence of a thesis, must write into existence a self that you will be comfortable inhabiting. The structure of the thesis affects each of the tasks that the thesis performs.

The dimensions of the work of structure have significance to some of the work of the thesis that is essentially social: enabling access; persuading a community of your own maturity and worthiness for responsibility; and creating a persona that is credible and creditable. Finding a final structure may be psychologically challenging because this is not just about good writing skills but about engaging and connecting with other people. If decisions have been hard for you to make, this is probably because the work behind the thesis matters to you, and because you care about how the people who read your thesis will receive you as an author. It is also possible that the deep-level values, the axiology of your discipline, your data and yourself (as a person rather than primarily as a professional) are affected by the structure of your thesis.

In this book, we have split comments on structuring a thesis into three sections covering order, emphasis and cohesion. We have used suggestions from a number of thesis-writing guides as well as our own, and stories from thesis writers including ourselves. The three strands of structure – order, emphasis and cohesion – also overlap to some extent. Although we feel that thinking about the mechanics of designing structure can be done best by thinking through these three lenses as a means of angling at precision, we do not mean to suggest that structural choices are merely mechanical. They are not: they are also socially situated. As with most social systems, there are covert rules behind writing that readers interpret as a semiotic system. Readers will think that more space on one topic makes it more important than parallel-level topics that were given less space. They will tend to focus on the first and the last, and to read the thesis as a narrative that progresses developmentally. What comes towards the end will therefore be seen as superseding what came earlier. Awareness of some of the covert working of structure will hopefully enable you to mechanically manipulate the semiotics of structure to suit the social tasks of the thesis.

We reiterate that theses usually require compromise. They are never really finished, but merely, their closure is negotiated. This is planet Earth, a place of imperfection. As fellow dwellers in such a place of negotiated compromise, we wish you strength and satisfaction in decisively shaping your thesis structure according to what really matters about your work.

Bibliography

J.L. Austin (1975) *How to do things with words* (Cambridge, MA: Harvard University Press).

J. Battista (2004) 'Me he korokoro [With the throat of a bellbird]: A Māori aesthetic in Māori writing in English', unpublished PhD thesis, University of Auckland.

T. Becher (1994) 'The significance of disciplinary differences', *Studies in Higher Education*, 19, 151–61.

T. Becher and P. Trowler (2001) *Academic tribes and territories: Intellectual enquiry and the culture of disciplines*, 2nd edn (Philadelphia: Open University Press).

C. Belsey (1994) *Desire: Love stories in Western culture* (Oxford: Blackwell).

D. Bleich (2001) 'The materiality of language and the pedagogy of exchange', *Pedagogy: Critical approaches to teaching literature, language, composition and culture*, 1, 117–41.

C. Booker (2004) *The seven basic plots: Why we tell stories* (London: Continuum).

R.S. Brause (2000) *Writing your doctoral dissertation: Invisible rules for success* (London: Falmer Press).

A.S. Byatt (1990) *Possession: A Romance* (London: Chatto & Windus).

S. Carter (2009) 'Old lamps for new: Mnemonic techniques and the thesis structure', *Arts and Humanities in Higher Education*, 8, 56–68.

S. Carter and M. Blumenstein (2011) 'Thesis structure: Student experience and attempts towards solution', conference paper presented at 34th Annual International HERDSA Conference, 4–7 July 2011.

F.L. Collins (2006) 'Learning to cross borders: Everyday urban encounters between South Korea and Auckland', unpublished PhD thesis, University of Auckland.

Dance your Ph.D (2011) Science AAAS. Accessed at http://gonzolabs.org/dance/, viewed 28 October 2011.

L. Davis and S. McKay (1996) *Structure and strategies: An introduction to academic writing* (South Yarra: Macmillan).

Department for Education and Skills (2007) *Bologna Process Stocktaking London 2007*, http://www.ond.vlaanderen.be/hogeronderwijs/bologna/documents/WGR2007/Stocktaking_report2007.pdf

P. Dunleavy (2003) *Authoring a PhD: How to plan, draft, write and finish a doctoral thesis or dissertation* (Basingstoke: Palgrave Macmillan).

N.L. Eik-Nes (2008) 'Front stage and back stage writing: Using logs to rehearse and develop a disciplinary role', *Nordic Journal of English Studies*, 7, 181–98.

A.A. Glatthorn (1998) *Writing the winning dissertation: A step-by-step guide* (Thousand Oaks: Corwin Press).

S. Johnston (1997) 'Examining the examiners: Analysis of examiners' reports on doctoral theses', *Studies in Higher Education*, 22, 333–47.

B. Kamler and P. Thomson (2006) *Helping doctoral students write: Pedagogies for supervision* (London: Routledge).

F. Kelly (2002) 'In "that Borderland Between": The ambivalence of A.S. Byatt's fiction', unpublished PhD thesis, University of Auckland.

H.B. Laurenson (2003) 'Going up? Going down! The rise and fall of Auckland department stores, 1920–1960', unpublished MA thesis, University of Auckland.

J.C. Lockhart (1997) 'Towards a theory of the configuration and management of export-dependent land-based value systems: The case of New Zealand', unpublished PhD thesis, University of Auckland.

R. Madigan, S. Johnson, and P. Linton. (1995) 'The language of psychology: APA style as epistemology', *American Psychologist*, 6, 428–36.

D. Madsen (1988) *Successful dissertations and theses* (San Francisco: Jossey-Bass).

E. Manalo and J. Trafford (2004) *Thinking to thesis: A guide to graduate success at all levels* (Auckland: Pearson Longman).

T. Maua-Hodges (2000) *Ako Pai Ki Aitutaki: Transporting or weaving cultures, Research report of field experiences to the Cook Islands* (Wellington: Wellington College of Education).

N. Moore (2000) *How to do research: The complete guide to designing and managing research projects* (London: Library Association Publishing).

G. Mullins and M. Kiley (2002) '"It's a PhD, not a Nobel Prize": How experienced examiners assess research theses', *Studies in Higher Education*, 27, 369–86.

R. Murray (2011) *How to write a thesis*, 3rd edn (Maidenhead: Open University Press).

U. Nabobo (2003) 'Indigenous Fijian educational ideas' in K.H. Thaman (ed.), *Educational ideas from Oceania: Selected readings*, pp. 85–93 (Suva: University of the South Pacific).

J.D. Novak (1998) *Learning, creating and using knowledge: Concept maps as facilitative tools in schools and universities* (Mahwah, NJ: Lawrence Erlbaum).

L. Parker (2004) 'Qualitative research' in S. Burton and P. Stearn (eds), *Surviving your thesis*, pp. 159–77 (London: Routledge).

S. Parry (2007) *Disciplines and doctorates* (Dordrecht: Springer).

B.T. Pentland (1999) 'Building process theory with narrative: From description to explanation', *Academy of Management Review*, 24, 711–24.

E.M. Phillips and D.S. Pugh (2010) *How to get a PhD: A handbook for students and their supervisors*, 3rd edn (Philadelphia: Open University Press).

E. Rankin (2001) *The work of writing: Insights and strategies for academics and professionals* (San Francisco: Jossey-Bass).

L. Richardson (1990) *Writing strategies: Reaching diverse audiences* (Thousand Oaks, CA: Sage Qualitative Methodology Series).

K. Rountree and T. Laing (1996) *Writing by degrees: A practical guide to writing theses and research papers* (Auckland: Longman).

K.E. Rudestam and R.R. Newton (2001) *Surviving your dissertation: A comprehensive guide to content and process*, 2nd edn (Thousand Oaks, CA: Sage).

G. Rugg and M. Petre (2005) *The unwritten rules of PhD research* (Maidenhead: Open University Press).

D. Sternberg (1981) *How to complete and survive a doctoral dissertation* (New York: St. Martin's Press).

E. Stokes (1985) *Māori research and development: A discussion paper* (Hamilton: University of Waikato).

S.R. Sturm (2008) 'Chamier the Epicurean: The life and works of George Chamier (1842–1915)', unpublished PhD thesis, University of Auckland.

D. Swetnam (2003) *Writing your dissertation*, 3rd edn (Oxford: How to Books).

H. Sword (2007) *The Writer's Diet* (Auckland: Pearson).

R.M. Thomas and D.L. Brubaker (2000) *Theses and dissertations: A guide to planning, research, and writing* (Westport, CT: Greenwood).

V. Trafford and S. Leshem (2002) 'Starting at the end to undertake doctoral research: Predictable questions as stepping stones', *Higher Education Review*, 34, 43–61.

University of Auckland (2011) *Statute and Guidelines for the Degree of Doctor of Philosophy*, University of Auckland.

L. Wallace (1996) 'Tryst tropique: Pacific texts, modern sexualities', unpublished PhD thesis, University of Auckland.

I. Watt (1987) *The rise of the novel: Studies in Defoe, Richardson and Fielding* (London: Hogarth).

B. White (2011) *Mapping your thesis: Techniques and rhetorics for masters' and doctoral researchers* (Camberwell: ACER).

J.M. White (2007) 'Spirit of the passion: topoi of belief in the McCahon canon', unpublished PhD thesis, University of Auckland.

J.M. Williams (1997) *Style: Ten lessons in clarity and grace*, 5th edn (New York: Longman).

G. Wisker (2008) *The postgraduate research handbook: Succeed with your MA, MPhil, EdD and PhD*, 2nd edn (Basingstoke: Palgrave Macmillan).

F.A. Yates (1966) *The art of memory* (Aylesbury: Watson & Viney).

Index